The Water and the Wine

A Contribution to the Debate on Children and Holy Communion

Roger Beckwith and
Andrew Daunton-Fear

The Latimer Trust

The Water and the Wine:
A Contribution to the Debate on Children and Holy Communion

ISBN 0 946307 54 7

Published by the Latimer Trust
PO Box 26685
London N14 4XQ

www.latimertrust.org

CONTENTS

Foreword by The Bishop Of Rochester

Roger Beckwith and Andrew Daunton-Fear are to be congratulated for producing this closely argued monograph. They are protagonists for maintaining the traditional Anglican pattern of baptism–confirmation and reception of communion. Their concerns relate particularly to seeing Christian initiation as process, especially where infants are baptised, and they see confirmation, with the receiving of communion, as a climax to this process. They are also, of course, concerned that confirmation should flourish in a church which practises infant baptism, as it can be a key moment in making a personal declaration of faith.

It should be noted that the House of Bishops guidelines on the admission of baptised persons to holy communion, before confirmation, continue to hold to the 'inherited norm' promoted by the two authors. Any dispensation from it is ultimately derived from Canon B15A which allows those who are 'ready and desirous' for confirmation to receive communion. It is for this reason that the guidelines insist on children, receiving communion before confirmation, being able to appreciate the significance of the sacraments.

In keeping with the guidelines, in the diocese of Rochester, we insist that parishes seeking dispensation from the norm should ensure that the reception of holy communion by children should be part of a process leading up to confirmation. It is necessary to put such safeguards in place if confirmation is not to 'wither on the vine' in these situations.

The authors point out that there is an irreducible tension between maintaining the Anglican norm of baptism – confirmation – communion and the guideline that a baptised person, child or adult, who has once been admitted to communion should not anywhere be deprived of it. I can only say that the House of Bishops was, after a time, aware of this tension but hoped that it could be resolved pastorally.

We are taken at a canter through Jewish antecedents in respect of proselyte baptism and the celebration of the Passover. The authors point out the significance of the age of discretion for the latter. There is a good discussion of the origins and development of the practice of the post-baptismal laying-on of hands (though some further material on anointing would have been welcome). The Reformers' insistence on a later age for both confirmation and first communion is also well-documented.

They are right to remind us that the pioneers of the Evangelical movement were among the first to promote the frequent celebration and reception of communion. There should, therefore, be a continuing commitment to eucharistic provision at a time which is accessible to the majority but also to non-eucharistic provision, especially for those who are on the fringes of church life. If Family Communion continues to be the main provision on a Sunday morning, this does not necessarily exclude children from other kinds of instruction and even worship. Some thought, however, needs to be given generally to teaching both adults and children in ways that lead to deeper faith and wider knowledge.

Each of the chapters in this brief work is stimulating in its own right. Whatever people's opinion may be on this matter, they should take account of what Roger and Andrew have to say. I commend their work for study and reflection in the Church.

Bishop Michael Nazir-Ali

September 2003

About the Authors

Roger Beckwith, after curacies in the Chelmsford and Bristol dioceses, taught Liturgy first at Tyndale Hall, Bristol, then at Wycliffe Hall, Oxford, and has also looked after two Oxfordshire parishes. He was successively Librarian and Warden of Latimer House, and has published many articles and some books, chiefly relating to Intertestamental Judaism, Liturgy and Anglican doctrine and practice. In 1992 he was awarded a Lambeth D.D. His chapters in the present volume look at the Jewish background to Christian practice and at the approach of the Anglican Reformers to baptism, confirmation and admission to communion.

Andrew Daunton-Fear has served as a parish priest for twenty-four years, first in the diocese of Peterborough, then in the diocese of Rochester. In 1976 he received a B.Phil. (St Andrews), and in 2000 a Ph.D. (London), both in the field of Patristics. He now teaches at St Andrew's Episcopal Seminary in Manila. It was the publication of the 'Knaresborough' report that first aroused his concern, particularly its perceived threat to confirmation, which he had learnt to value greatly as an opportunity to bring young and adult candidates to a commitment to Christ. In his chapters in this book on the New Testament evidence and on the Early Church, he questions the contention that water baptism is full sacramental initiation for infants and considers related issues.

The contributors make no claim to pronounce the final word on the aspects of the subject they address, but they do wish to show that there is another side to the debate, not simply that which has received almost all the publicity in recent years, and that the pattern traditional in the Church of England since the Reformation may be upheld with integrity. Though they have discussed their work together, and consulted others, ultimate responsibility for the views they express in their individual chapters is theirs alone. The chapter on Pastoral Considerations is the joint work of the two authors.

Acknowledgements

We wish to thank Dr Katherine Kaye, who discussed our project with us at many stages; Dr Graham Gould of King's College, London, Professor Anthony Thiselton of Nottingham University, and Professor David Wright of Edinburgh University, who read individual chapters and made helpful suggestions; and Dr Michael Nazir-Ali, bishop of Rochester, who kindly wrote the foreword to the book. For help in the preparation of the typescript, we are indebted to Lindsay Taylor.

CHAPTER ONE
INTRODUCTION

The age of admission to communion is one of those questions on which the New Testament gives no direct guidance, and which the church is therefore left to decide on general biblical principles. As in other such cases, it has not always or everywhere made the same decision. The earliest period is the most obscure, though inferences can be drawn from the New Testament and Judaism. From the middle of the third century onwards, we know of three different ages of admission: infancy, childhood and adolescence. The Western Church at that time had begun to opt for infancy: by the latter part of the fourth century the same practice had evidently developed in the East, and it has continued there ever since. In the thirteenth century, the Western Church had second thoughts, and moved admission to childhood, when consciousness had dawned and a degree of preparation was feasible. Then in the sixteenth century, at the Reformation of the Western Church, the reformed churches (including the Church of England) moved the age again, this time to adolescence, so as to make more adequate preparation possible, with an invitation to personal Christian commitment.

After more than 400 years, during most of which a stable pattern of Christian initiation has prevailed in the Church of England and been followed in the Anglican Communion abroad, there has in the last thirty years or so been a move in a different direction.

The historic Anglican pattern consisted of the baptism, in infancy, of the children of professing Christian parents, followed by their confirmation by the bishop at the 'age of discretion' (about twelve to fifteen years), after a course of instruction on the lines of the Prayer Book Catechism. At their confirmation they would take upon themselves the vows of repentance, faith and obedience, made on their behalf at their baptism, and would be admitted to holy communion.

The authors believe that this historic pattern is still the best, recognising as it does the importance of understanding as a normal pre-requisite for worthily receiving communion, and also the need to complete baptism by personal repentance and faith, and to express this publicly, before going on to public participation in the sacrament of maturity, the Lord's Supper. They repudiate the idea that infant baptism, as an external ordinance, is complete in itself, and automatically entitles the candidate to receive the other sacrament.

The Parish Communion movement, which began in Anglo-Catholic circles before the Second World War, but subsequently extended its influence considerably, in recent years established a celebration of communion as the main Sunday service in most parish churches, replacing Morning or Evening Prayer. As a result, many children, who might otherwise have been at Sunday School, started coming with their parents to the communion rail. In order to include them, it became customary that, while their confirmed parents received the bread and wine, they received a blessing, like the children blessed by our Lord (Mark 10:13-16). Though many children were content, some protested (or their parents on their behalf) that they were not sharing in the sacred meal. So, aware that Orthodox children communicated from the time of their baptism in infancy, and that Roman Catholic children normally took their first communion at about seven, and with members of the World Council of Churches urging a reconsideration of the matter by Protestants in the interests of ecumenical rapprochement, some Anglicans began to look again at the traditional pattern.

An obstacle to change was insistence on the importance of confirmation, and this had been bolstered since the late-nineteenth century by certain Anglo-Catholic theologians who had claimed that confirmation played an essential role in the reception of the Holy Spirit, and so was in effect a sacrament necessary to salvation. These claims had been powerfully contested in Geoffrey Lampe's book *The Seal of the Spirit*[1] and as a result of this controversy the real importance of confirmation had tended to be obscured in people's minds.

The scene was therefore set for the 'Ely' report *Christian Initiation: Birth and Growth in the Christian Society*,[2] which declared that baptism is complete sacramental initiation and is sufficient basis for admitting children to communion prior to confirmation. Though this report was not endorsed by the General Synod, and was particularly strongly opposed by the bishops, who feared the effect of the new theory on numbers coming to confirmation (their main point of contact with the laity of their dioceses), it was later followed by the 'Knaresborough' report *Communion before Confirmation?*, which presented the same proposals. This report included a review of the situation in other denominations and other Anglican Churches, and incidentally revealed the alarming effect of the new practice on numbers offering for confirmation in New Zealand.[3]

The Anglican Consultative Council, meeting at Singapore in 1987, expressed the strongest reservations about the new practice,[4] but the Fourth International Anglican Liturgical Consultation, meeting at Toronto in 1991, supported it.[5] Meanwhile, a series of Grove Booklets was seeking to remove objections, some writers advocating the Roman Catholic age of admission and some the Eastern Orthodox.[6]

---

[1] Geoffrey W.H. Lampe, *The Seal of the Spirit: A Study in the Doctrine of Baptism and Confirmation in the New Testament and the Fathers* (London: SPCK, 1951),

[2] *Christian Initiation: Birth and Growth in the Christian Society* (London: CIO, 1971).

[3] *Communion before Confirmation?*, 'Knaresborough' report (London: CIO, 1985), p. 64.

[4] *Many Gifts, One Spirit* (London: Church House Publishing, 1987), pp. 68-71.

[5] David Holeton (ed.), *Christian Initiation in the Anglican Communion: The Toronto Statement 'Walk in Newness of Life'* (Grove Worship Series 118, 1991).

[6] Christopher Byworth, *Communion, Confirmation and Commitment* (Grove Worship Series 8, 1972); David Holeton, *Infant Communion Then and Now* (Grove Liturgical Study 27, 1981); Colin Buchanan, *Anglican Confirmation* (Grove Liturgical Study 48, 1986); Colin Buchanan, *Children in Communion* (Grove Worship Series

The tide was now beginning to flow, and in 1996 the House of Bishops produced for General Synod a report *Admission to Communion in relation to Baptism and Confirmation*,[7] setting out guidelines for the admission of baptised children to communion before confirmation, at the Roman Catholic not the Orthodox age – an age when the child had an 'appreciation of the significance of the sacrament'. It said that children so admitted in one parish must not be refused admission in any other parish. Significantly, however, the report declared that the traditional sequence should continue to be regarded as the 'normal practice in our Church', communion before confirmation being a departure from the inherited norm and therefore requiring special permission. A report of developments since, published by the Education Division in 2005 (*Children and Holy Communion: A Review*),[8] shows that most bishops have now permitted the new practice in at least one church, and four bishops in a hundred or more, but that in the country as a whole the proportion of churches participating amounts only to 9%.

A few voices had, in fact, been heard in favour of the traditional Anglican position. Articles were written, including those by the authors of the present volume[9] and an earlier Latimer Study addressed the issue.[10] That there is a substantial case, both theological and practical, in favour of

112, 1990); Mark Dalby, *Infant Communion: the New Testament to the Reformation* (Alcuin-Grove Joint Liturgical Study 56, 2003).

[7] House of Bishops, *Admission to Communion in relation to Baptism and Confirmation* (London: GS 1212, 1996).

[8] Education Division, 'Children and Holy Communion: A Review' (London: GS 1576, 2005).

[9] Roger Beckwith, 'The Age of Admission to Communion', *Churchman* 85:1 (Spring 1971); Roger Beckwith, 'The Age of Admission to the Lord's Supper', *Westminster Theological Journal* 38:2 (Winter 1976); Roger Beckwith, *Communion before Confirmation* (Latimer Comment 50, 1993); Andrew Daunton-Fear, 'Resisting the Tide: Christian Initiation and Communion Reconsidered', *Theology* 98 (July/August 1995). The second title was a reply to an article by C.L. Keidel, 'Is the Lord's Supper for Children?', *Westminster Theological Journal* 37:1 (Spring 1975), which gave rise to considerable discussion among American Presbyterians.

[10] A.A. Langdon, *Communion for Children? The Current Debate* (Latimer Study 28, 1988). This argues, on educational grounds, that children do not understand symbolism until about the age of 12. It drew a reply, on different grounds, from G.N. Davies: 'The Lord's Supper for the Lord's Children', *Reformed Theological Review* 50:1 (1991).

the traditional pattern, which is not at present being seriously considered, is the conviction that has motivated the writing of this book.

CHAPTER TWO
THE JEWISH BACKGROUND TO CHRISTIAN PRACTICE

There are certain clear similarities in ceremonial between Old Testament and Intertestamental Judaism on the one hand and New Testament Christianity on the other. Though the Jewish ceremonial is elaborate and the Christian simple, they both have an initiation ceremony and they both have a regular sacred meal.

The original initiation ceremony of Judaism was circumcision, a rite for males only, whereas the initiation ceremony of Christianity is baptism, a rite for both sexes. The command to perform circumcision was first given to Abraham, the archetypal man of faith (Genesis 15:6; 17:10-14), and Paul calls it a seal of the righteousness of his faith (Romans 4:11), but nevertheless the command was from the outset extended to the week-old children of adult believers. The question arises whether baptism, which the New Testament closely links with faith (Acts 19:4-7; Galatians 3:25-29; Colossians 2:12), was from the beginning similarly extended to believers' infant children.

The most important of the sacred meals of Judaism was the Passover meal, of which the circumcised alone might partake (Exodus 12:43-49). It was observed only once a year, which is hardly surprising in view of the number of other sacred meals and ceremonies which the Law of Moses enjoined; but the holy communion, which was instituted at the Passover season, and is similarly a commemoration of redemption, has always been observed much more frequently (Acts 20:7). It is observed among those who have been baptised (Acts 2:41-47; see also 1 Corinthians 10:1-4), just as the Passover meal was observed among the circumcised.

The Jewish Practice of Initiation

In the middle decades of the twentieth century a great debate took place, especially on the continent but also in Britain, on whether infant baptism is of apostolic origin. This was, of course, the revival of a much older debate, and as before it reached no certain conclusion, partly because too many of the participants were committed in advance to a particular answer. One of the participants was Karl Barth, who seldom wrote about the sacraments, but vigorously opposed infant baptism on theological grounds. Most of the participants, however, attempted to approach the question historically, and the debate involved the study not only of the New Testament and the Fathers, but also of Judaism. Here, it was the exceptional Jewish learning of Joachim Jeremias that gave him an advantage over other participants. Jeremias argued that infant baptism began in the time of the apostles. No doubt some of his opinions are disputable, and he did overstate his case, unduly minimising the third and fourth-century patristic evidence for a delay of baptism, except in emergencies; but in the area of Jewish studies he made out a very powerful case, which provided a compelling first-century background to the statements of the New Testament. His book *Infant Baptism in the First Four Centuries* was answered by Kurt Aland, but Jeremias came back with a crushing rejoinder in *The Origins of Infant Baptism.*[11] Jeremias makes much of the fact that, in the case of Gentile converts, the Pharisees had added to circumcision

---

[11] Joachim Jeremias, *Kindertaufe in den ersten vier Jahrhunderten* (1958), translated as *Infant Baptism in the First Four Centuries* (London: SCM, 1960); Kurt Aland, *Die Säuglingstaufe im Neuen Testament und in der Alten Kirche* (1961), translated as *Did the Early Church Baptise Infants?* (London: SCM, 1963); Joachim Jeremias, *Nochmals: die Anfänge der Kindertaufe* (1962), translated as *The Origins of Infant Baptism* (London: SCM, 1963). The patristic scholar David Wright reviewed the debate between Jeremias and Aland in 'The Origins of Infant Baptism – Child Believers' Baptism?', *Scottish Journal of Theology* 40 (1987), pp. 1-23. He conceded the existence of infant baptism in the late second and early third centuries, but he suggested that it might have originated as an extension of child believers' baptism. A similar view, that it originated from baptism in emergency, had earlier been proposed by Everett Ferguson, 'Inscriptions and the Origin of Infant Baptism', *Journal of Theological Studies* 30 (1979), pp. 37-46. These theories, of course, assume that infant baptism does not go back to the beginning, as Jeremias had argued.

a rite known as proselyte baptism, which was also suitable for use with female proselytes, of any age.

At the beginning of the Christian era, Pharisaism was the largest and most influential school of religious thought among the Jews, as Josephus and the Mishnah alike report. Even in the Temple, where the Sadducean high priesthood held sway, the views of the Pharisees were nonetheless influential, because of the popular support they enjoyed. Pharisaism was also a missionary movement, as Jesus noted in a very sharp saying (Matthew 23:15). Because of their preoccupation with ceremonial cleansing, the Pharisees had added to the requirements for conversion to Judaism a cleansing rite designed to wash away all the manifold ceremonial uncleanness which the convert had incurred during his Gentile life.[12] The Mishnah shows that this rite was taken for granted in the disputes between the Pharisaic schools of Shammai and Hillel in the first century A.D., following the deaths of Shammai and Hillel themselves a generation earlier (Pesahim 8:8; Eduyoth 5:2). Therefore it must predate the Christian era. The schools disputed whether the rite needed to be performed a day before or a week before the Passover, in order to cleanse a proselyte in time to eat of the lamb.

Further evidence of the antiquity of the rite is provided by the Greek Testament of Levi 14:6, where Levi says that his decadent descendants 'will take the daughters of the Gentiles to wife, purifying them with an unlawful purification'.[13] This work has Essene tendencies, and though the Essenes shared the Pharisaic emphasis on ceremonial cleansing, they were strongly opposed to intermarriage with

---

[12] Some rabbis held a sophisticated view that Gentiles, not being under the Law, were not liable to become ceremonially unclean, but the two early pieces of evidence at which we are about to look assume the straightforward view that they were so liable, which also underlies the standard practice of proselyte baptism.
[13] Antecedents of several of the Testaments of the Twelve Patriarchs, in Aramaic or Hebrew, have been found at Qumran, supplementing what had already been found in the Cairo Genizah. The Greek text is a very free version, but there is no good reason to question the old view that the paraphrast was a pre-Christian Jew, to whose work, after it had passed into the possession of Christians (presumably in the first century), certain Christian interpolations were added.

Gentiles, and are here accusing Pharisees of using proselyte baptism to facilitate it.

A third indication of the antiquity of proselyte baptism is the likelihood that John's baptism developed out of it. Proselyte baptism is closely linked with the cleansing rites of the Old Testament, of which it is a new application, both aimed at washing away ceremonial uncleanness. John's baptism, on the other hand, is closely linked with Christian baptism, of which it is the forerunner, both aimed at washing away not ceremonial uncleanness but moral uncleanness, that is, sin. The point of contact between the two pairs of ceremonies is that John's baptism, like proselyte baptism, is an initiation rite, performed once only at the time of conversion. John reinterpreted proselyte baptism as a washing away of sin, and therefore applied it to Jews as much as Gentiles, but likewise in an initiatory fashion.

Proselyte baptism had the advantage that, unlike circumcision, it was applicable to women. The rite was also applicable to children, of either sex, because children, as the Mishnah indicates, were likewise liable to contract ceremonial uncleanness (Tohoroth 3:6; Niddah 5:3-5; Zabim 2:1), and there is no record that proselyte baptism was ever denied to children.

The addition of proselyte baptism to circumcision in Jewish initiation practice was a significant step in the direction of what was to be Christian practice. Outwardly, circumcision was quite unlike baptism, and it was confined to the male sex. In its meaning, however, circumcision had a strong similarity to baptism, because both were initiation rites, and because circumcision had been spiritualised by the Old Testament as circumcision of the heart. Circumcision of the heart, when performed by the man himself, corresponds to repentance (Leviticus 26:41; Deuteronomy 10:16; Jeremiah 4:4; 9:26; Ezekiel 44:7, 9), which the New Testament links with Christian baptism (Acts 2:38). When performed by God, circumcision of the heart corresponds to regeneration (Deuteronomy 30:6), which the New

Testament again links with Christian baptism (John 3:5; Titus 3:5). The explicit connection which Paul makes between spiritual circumcision and Christian baptism in Colossians 2:11-14 is therefore only to be expected. And when a baptism rite, applicable to both sexes, was added by the Jews to circumcision, an outward similarity to what was to be Christian baptism was joined to the existing inner similarity. The claim made by Baptist writers that circumcision does not have any clear likeness to Christian baptism is therefore rather short-sighted.[14]

There is one interesting difference between circumcision and proselyte baptism which may have affected early Christian practice. Circumcision was given in every generation. Proselyte baptism, however, was given only in the first generation, after which the proselyte and his family would observe the laws of ceremonial cleanness, and so would not need to repeat it. On this model, a Christian family might be baptised in every generation or only in the first generation, and it is possible that there was for a time a variety of practice among Christians. Baptism in every generation, of course, prevailed, and this was appropriate, since Christian baptism was concerned not with the observance of ceremonial cleanness but with the forgiveness of sins (Acts 2:38; 22:16) and the gift of the Holy Spirit (John 3:5; Acts 2:38; Titus 3:5), which every Christian needs individually and can only receive from the hands of God.

We have explicit evidence that circumcision and proselyte baptism were given to infants as well as adults. In the case of John's baptism and Christian baptism, the New Testament evidence is not explicit and we are dependant upon inference. But if John's baptism was an adaptation of proselyte baptism, one may assume that he too would probably have admitted the infant children of his converts, and the more so as he was baptising in immediate expectation of divine judgment on those who did not respond to his message (Matthew 3:7-12; Luke 3:7-17). A

[14] A claim which, surprisingly, is echoed by David Wright in his article (pp. 18-20).

similar inference could be made in the case of Christian baptism, and here we have a little more to go on, because there are the records of converts whose households or families were baptised with themselves. The first of these is apparently the God-fearer Cornelius at Caesarea (Acts 10:1-2, 46-48; 11:14). Then there are various instances in Macedonia and Greece: the God-fearer Lydia (Acts 16:14-15), the Philippian jailor (Acts 16:33), the Jew Crispus (Acts 18:8) and Stephanas (1 Corinthians 1:16). It is hard to think that, in the cases of Jews and God-fearers, when their households were baptised, this would not have included any children they had, in accordance with Jewish practice. In the cases of Gentile converts, there might be more room for doubt, but in these cases too, of course, the apostles supervising their baptism were Jews.

But though we may have some confidence that infant baptism began in the apostolic age, we cannot be sure that it was at first universal. We have noted the possibility that in some Jewish families it was not practised except in the first generation, and that in some Gentile families there was less readiness for it than in Jewish. If this is so, there was probably a variety of practice until agreement was reached that every Christian needed to be baptised. This would still leave open the question, at what age he needed to be baptised. Infant baptism was now doubtless widely practised, as the evidence of Irenaeus, Tertullian and Hippolytus (from the late second and early third centuries) indicates, but the numerous converts from paganism were still baptised as adults, which made it possible for Tertullian to raise the question whether this was not a better age for baptism. He did not claim that infant baptism was a novelty,[15] but he argued that the forgiveness of sins was less needed in infancy: it was more suitable at an age when there were actual sins to be repented and washed away, and when the candidate was capable of faith (*On Baptism* 18). Others

[15] As David Wright perceptively notes (p. 7). Tertullian's reference to the sponsors of infant candidates (*On Baptism* 18) shows that infant baptism was a well-established practice, and in his later work *On the Soul* (ch. 39) he seems to accept the practice as normal.

thought similarly, to judge from third-century inscriptions which show baptism sometimes delayed until there was danger of death.[16] And after the conversion of the Empire in the fourth century, such delay became for a time, though only for a time, common. A fruitless attempt to avoid post-baptismal sin seems to have been the reason.

At the conversion of the Empire there was naturally a flood of adult converts, but it was not long before almost all adults were at least nominal Christians, and were baptised as such, and the only remaining candidates for baptism were the children who might be born to them, in that or succeeding generations. While the practice of delaying baptism still existed, this did not make infant baptism universal, but it was simply a matter of time before it did. Only in missionary work in new lands or among new peoples would the situation be any different.

The Jewish Passover Meal

The Jewish background to the holy communion is the Passover meal. Jesus instituted the holy communion when he went up to Jerusalem for the Passover festival, and most scholars think that he instituted it at the actual Passover meal which commenced the festival, as the Synoptic Gospels seem to say. Jeremias, who is once again the leading authority on the matter, points out that in the Fourth Gospel also the Last Supper has many of the features of the Passover meal, but the chronology of the Gospel creates a problem.[17] He believes that John has altered the chronology for symbolic reasons, but it is perhaps more likely that John assumes a knowledge of one or more of the Synoptic Gospels in his readers, and intends his own statements to be interpreted accordingly. At all events, the holy communion was instituted at the Passover season, and should be understood against that background.

---

[16] Ferguson, 'Inscriptions and the Origin of Infant Baptism'.

[17] Joachim Jeremias, *Die Abendmahlsworte Jesu* (3rd edition, 1960), translated as *The Eucharistic Words of Jesus* (London: SCM, 1966).

We tend to think of the Passover meal as the Bible describes it in Egypt, or as it takes place today in a Jewish home. We think of it as a domestic event, for the whole family, based upon a sacrificed lamb, or now upon an ordinary joint of meat. We easily forget that, in the centuries after the Exodus, and right up to the destruction of the Temple by the Romans, it involved a journey to the sanctuary, where alone the offering of sacrifice was permitted. It was one of the three pilgrim feasts, when all male Israelites were bidden to present themselves before the Lord (Exodus 23:17; 34:23; Deuteronomy 16:16), and the meal was to be eaten by the pilgrims in or around the Temple court – it was no longer possible in Jesus' day, as in biblical times, to confine it to the Temple court, because of the numbers, so it took place in borrowed rooms throughout the holy city of Jerusalem.

The Mishnah is quite clear about the distinction between the Passover of Egypt and the Passover of the Generations (Pesahim 9:5). The claim that circumcised boys (if ceremonially clean) had a right to partake of the Passover meal, and that baptised children therefore have a right to partake of the holy communion, ignores the distinction between the Passover of Egypt and the Passover of the Generations. Circumcised boys who had been weaned certainly had the right to partake of the Passover of Egypt, because they were commanded to (Exodus 12:4, 'according to the number of the souls'), and the right presumably extended to the women and girls of the household as well; but the Passover of the Generations, being a pilgrim feast for male Israelites, was an individual rather than a family responsibility. It is true that the Pharisees (but not the Essenes) drew an analogy with the Passover of Egypt that allowed them to admit women and children as well as men, but this was only a permission: it is not clear that it carried either a right or a responsibility, so it could not extend any right or responsibility to Christians.

Thus, the Passover of Egypt, far from being the norm for all Passovers, as the Last Supper is for all eucharists, was in fact unique. Never again would the Passover sacrifice be eaten in the worshippers' own houses, with blood sprinkled round the entrance. On the contrary, it would be eaten in tents until the Tabernacle was erected, and, from then right up until the destruction of the Second Temple, it would be eaten in or around the sanctuary. As soon as the people entered the promised land, it became a pilgrim feast, and was celebrated far from most Israelites' homes. It was the Passover of the Generations which Jesus was celebrating at the Last Supper. If he had wanted to take the thoughts of his disciples back to the Passover of Egypt instead, as Christian Keidel and his followers apparently suppose that he did, he would have celebrated it standing and not reclining, and he would have avoided the use of wine, to say nothing of other changes. In fact, except in his interpretative words over the bread and the cup, he conformed to custom, and he even gave the wine a new importance.

Although the obligation of the Passover rested only upon men, we know from Josephus that women also were allowed to partake (*Jewish Antiquities* 11:4:8, or 11:109f; *Jewish War* 6:9:3, or 6:426), and the Mishnah confirms this (Pesahim 8:1, 5, 7). In St Luke's narrative, Mary as well as Joseph goes up to Jerusalem every year for the Passover (Luke 2:41). Unleavened bread could be eaten at home, but the lamb nowhere except at the Temple.

Some minors were also allowed to partake. Josephus speaks of children as well as women doing so (*Jewish Antiquities* 11:4:8, or 11:109f.) and the Mishnah again confirms this (Pesahim 8:7; 10:4). But because they had not reached the age of responsibility, the *obligation* did not rest upon them, and the Mishnah forbids making up a Passover company exclusively of women, slaves and minors (Pesahim 8:7).

In the Essene tradition, the view evidently taken was that those who were not obliged to eat the Passover were not *allowed* to do so either, and the Book of Jubilees therefore confines it to men of twenty years old and upward (Jubilees

49:17). This was the age of accountability in the Law (Numbers 14:29-31; 32:11), and the Essenes made it, similarly, the age of discretion and responsibility (see also appendix to the Qumran Community Rule, 1QSa). To do so was reasonable enough, but the Pharisees considered that the age of discernment could be somewhat younger, and the Mishnah indicates that it was judged to be thirteen, when the observance of the Law became an individual obligation (Aboth 5:21; see also Niddah 5:6). From this age, therefore, every male was obliged to observe the Passover, but he might observe it earlier, and females might do so too.

The biblical literature, however, informs us of two further restrictions. Male participants needed to have been circumcised (Exodus 12:43-50), and all participants needed to be ceremonially clean (Numbers 9:9-14). The rabbinical literature informs us of two further restrictions. The first is that, according to the Mishnah, every member of a Passover company must have at least an olive's bulk of the lamb's flesh assigned to him; if he is incapable of eating an olive's bulk of the flesh, he cannot be included in a Passover company (Pesahim 8:3, 6, 7). It follows that an infant who was not yet capable of coping with solid food could not be included in a Passover company.[18] The normal age of weaning was then two years (Gittin 7:6), though 2 Maccabees 7:27 says three; and it seems likely from the Mishnah that a boy who, with or without his father's instruction, was capable of asking the questions about the meaning of the foodstuffs on the Passover table (Pesahim 10:4), would have been the youngest participant.

The other restriction is that even participants did not necessarily partake of the Passover wine. The Passover wine is first mentioned in the second century B.C. (Jubilees 49:6); it is not one of the instituted elements of the feast, like lamb, unleavened bread and bitter herbs (Exodus 12:8; Numbers 9:11). It is significant that *baraitas* (early quotations) in both

[18] This inference is confirmed by the early halakic midrash on the Book of Exodus, Mekilta (Pisha 3), when expounding the phrase 'according to the number of the souls' (Exodus 12:4).

Talmuds tell us that Rabbi Judah ben Ilai (c. 150 A.D.), who often represents the older view, protested against the strange idea, then gaining currency, that the Passover wine should be given to women and children. The *baraitas* refer to Rabbi Akiba and Rabbi Tarfon, in the generation before, as agreeing with him (Jerusalem Talmud, Pesahim 10:1; Babylonian Talmud, Pesahim 108b-109a).[19] The bold proposal against which he protests may have been a consequence of transferring the Passover meal to the home, where all the family would necessarily be present, after the destruction of the Temple. His reason for withholding wine from children was doubtless the teaching of Scripture that wine needs to be treated with discretion (Proverbs 20:1; 21:17; Isaiah 5:11-13; 56:10-12), since discretion is precisely what children lack, as the Mishnah recognises (Arakhin 1:1; Tohoroth 3:6; Makshirin 3:8; 6:1). His reason for withholding wine from women also, one fears, was the low view which many rabbis had, and which the Mishnah reflects, of the female character (Sotah 3:4; Aboth 1:5; Tohoroth 7:9).

In the time of Jesus, therefore, we have good reason to think that no infants would have been admitted as members of a Passover company, and that though certain children might have been included, they would probably not have been allowed the Passover wine, which was not one of the instituted elements of the meal. At the age of thirteen, however, all males would have started partaking of the meal, including the wine, because that was the age when it became an obligation upon them.

At the Last Supper, there were only adult males present. But in instituting the Christian Passover meal, the holy communion, Jesus gave a significant indication whom it was in future intended for, by making the wine for the first time one of the instituted elements. So it was intended for those

[19] Instead of wine, children were given roasted ears of corn, and nuts. Or they might be given (extra) pieces of unleavened bread (Tosephta, Pesahim 10:9): this was 'so that they will not fall asleep' (but will presumably be able to learn something of the meaning of what is taking place).

who were of an age to drink wine, namely, adults. Elsewhere, Jesus gives a grave warning against causing little ones to stumble (Mark 9:42), and he would probably have regarded giving alcohol to children as falling within the scope of this warning.[20]

Consequently, the emphatic teaching of St Paul that participants must examine themselves and 'discern the body' (1 Corinthians 11:27-34) should be given its full weight, as applying to all participants alike, and excluding those not yet old enough to fulfil such requirements. Also, Jesus' command 'Do this in remembrance of me' (Luke 22:19; 1 Corinthians 11:24-25) is presumably directed to those capable of understanding and remembering, which would not include infants. (Indeed the whole symbolism of the sacrament, with all due respect, surely excludes infants, who – as Clement of Alexandria remarks in another connection – are nourished by sucking, not by eating and drinking).[21]

But was the holy communion intended for women? Of course it was! Jesus' attitude to women was quite different from that of the rabbis. He conversed publicly with them, allowed them to accompany him on his travels, admitted them among his pupils, and made them the first witnesses of his resurrection. And St Paul is again in agreement with Jesus' attitude (Galatians 3:28 etc.). There is no actual evidence of women receiving the holy communion in the New Testament, but the explicit patristic evidence (as is possibly significant) starts at the same time as for infant baptism, in the last twenty years of the second century.[22] It is

---

[20] It is sometimes asked whether a small quantity of wine could do children any harm. Perhaps not (provided it was not habit-forming). But while the eucharist was still part of a substantial meal, whether the Passover meal or the agape (as it originally was), there is no reason to think that the quantity would have been small. At the Passover meal, according to the Mishnah, a minimum of four cups of wine must be drunk, and there is unlimited drinking between the earlier cups (Pesahim 10:1, 7). At the love-feast, drinking was moderate, Tertullian says (*Apology* 39), as it no doubt was, but what is moderate for an adult may easily be too much for a child.

[21] Clement of Alexandria, *Pedagogue* 1.6.36.

[22] See *Acts of Peter* and *Acts of Paul*, in Edgar Hennecke, *New Testament Apocrypha*, (English translation, London: Lutterworth, 1963-65), vol. 2, pp. 280, 372. See also Tertullian, *To his Wife* 2.4, 8.

the period when the Fathers first begin to leave us really extensive writings.

Against this background, Cyprian's practice, in the mid-third century, of giving communion not just to children but even to infants, was clearly a novelty. The reason Cyprian introduced it may lie in the fact that we find him elsewhere using the argument (later urged by Augustine and others in defence of infant communion) that according to John 6:53 the reception of holy communion is necessary to salvation.[23] If so, it was motivated by a special interpretation of John 6:53. Cyprian's practice, despite his great reputation, did not quickly find imitators, and only two further references to infant or child communion are known in the next century and a half, one in the West and one in the East, as against many references to infant baptism in both areas.[24] But by the late fourth century, whether for the same or some other reason, the new practice had started to be adopted in the East (see *Apostolic Constitutions* 8.12-13), and there it has continued.

Jewish 'Confirmation'?

Since the Middle Ages, a Jewish boy, when entering on his adult responsibilities at the age of thirteen, has taken part in a public ceremony known as the Bar Mizwah rite. This, in still more recent times, has sometimes been referred to as 'confirmation', because of a certain similarity to Christian (especially Protestant) confirmation.

The Jewish ceremony is not very old. But it is based upon a much older principle, that the age of adult religious responsibility, according to traditional (Pharisaic) ideas, is thirteen. In Kaufmann Kohler's article 'Bar Mizwah' in the *Jewish Encyclopedia*, he connects this, as others have done, with Jesus being taken up to the Passover by his parents at the age of twelve (Luke 2:41-43), in accordance with the

---

[23] Cyprian, *On the Lord's Prayer* 18. See also *Three Books of Testimonies against the Jews* 3.25f, though book 3 is no longer regarded as Cyprian's own work.
[24] For the Western reference, a fourth-century inscription from Sicily, see Jeremias, *Infant Baptism in the First Four Centuries*, p. 90.

mishnaic practice of preparing boys for their adult responsibilities a year or two in advance (Yoma 8:4). He also connects it with the boast of Josephus that he was already being consulted about points of the Law at the age of fourteen (*Life* 2, or 9). There has to be some doubt about these parallels, because St Luke gives no hint that this was the first time Jesus had accompanied his parents to the festival, and because Josephus, rather inconsistently, describes himself as being at the time 'no better than a child'. However, the main point, that the age of responsibility for fulfilling the commandments was thirteen, is unaffected.

Any idea that the Bar Mizwah rite goes back to the beginning of the Christian era, and that Christian confirmation could have been modelled upon it, is an anachronism, and to this extent the belief of the Reformers that their confirmation practice agreed with Judaism and the early church was mistaken. Where, however, they were probably right was in believing that, in the earliest Christian times, before the innovation of Cyprian, the age of admission to communion was much the same as the age for fulfilling the commandments (including the Passover commandment) among the Jews, namely, about thirteen. There is little Christian evidence on this point from before the time of Cyprian, but what there is seems to bear it out.[25]

[25] See Origen, *Homilies on Judges* 6.2, and the Syrian *Didascalia Apostolorum* 9, in the passage beginning 'Honour the bishops ...' Compare also Clement of Alexandria, *Pedagogue* 2.2.20, where, after speaking of the eucharist, he emphasises how unsuitable wine is for boys and girls, and the importance of their avoiding it. Some of the material in this chapter overlaps with material in Roger Beckwith, *Calendar, Chronology and Worship: Studies in Ancient Judaism and Early Christianity* (Leiden: Brill, 2005), ch. 13.

CHAPTER THREE
THE NEW TESTAMENT EVIDENCE

In this chapter we shall examine the New Testament evidence to see what bearing it has on the subject of children and communion. We need not dwell here on infant baptism. In the previous chapter a strong case has been made from the Jewish evidence for the practice of infant baptism in the Church from earliest times (albeit not universally adhered to). Even supporters of believer's baptism agree this possibility cannot be excluded.[26]

Our task here will be rather, first to test the validity of the common assertion that baptism, including *infant* baptism, constitutes complete sacramental initiation and therefore sufficient grounds for admission to communion.[27] Secondly, we shall consider the major New Testament metaphors and images for baptism to see how legitimate it is to apply them to baptised infants. Thirdly, we shall look again at the laying on of hands within Christian initiation. Finally, we shall focus upon an important prerequisite stipulated by St Paul for those intending to receive communion.

Baptism as 'Complete Christian Initiation'

In the second edition of his classic study, *The Seal of the Spirit*, G.W.H. Lampe asserts that, 'Baptism is the sacrament of the whole gospel' – it brings salvation, it is the means whereby one receives Jesus Christ as Lord, it confers the Spirit – 'Nothing, therefore, can be added to what is given in

[26] For example, see the ecumenical document *Baptism, Eucharist and Ministry* (Geneva: World Council of Churches, 1982), p. 4.
[27] *Communion before Confirmation?*, 'Knaresborough' report, 2:1; 2:4:2; *Christian Initiation in the Anglican Communion*, 'Toronto Statement', 1:10 etc.

Baptism ... Confirmation is a *confirmation* of the baptismal gift.'[28]

But the truth is that the evidence of the New Testament (and indeed of the Fathers) is not entirely straightforward. Texts can be found which associate the gift of the indwelling Spirit with (water) baptism (Acts 2:38, 1 Corinthians 12:13), with the laying on of hands (Acts 8:17, 19:6), and with neither (Acts 10:44). The three Pauline texts which refer to 'sealing' the Christian (2 Corinthians 1:22, Ephesians 1:13, 4:30) mention neither baptism nor any other physical act but merely, as Lampe himself admits, 'the presence and activity of the indwelling Spirit of God'.[29] In discussing the Acts of the Apostles he laments Luke's 'apparently inconsistent account of Baptism in the apostolic age', seeing it as the source of 'the most acute theological problems which have beset the relationship of Baptism to Confirmation in the course of the Church's history.'[30] Subsequently, however, the more nimble-footed J.D.G. Dunn has made considerable sense of these apparent inconsistencies. In his study *Baptism in the Holy Spirit* he sees Acts 2:38 as a blueprint of Christian 'conversion-initiation', a complex consisting of three elements:

a) the act of faith of the initiate – described throughout Acts by one or more of the terms 'repentance', 'turning to (God)' or 'putting one's faith in (Christ)'

b) the response of the Christian community – water baptism

c) the supernatural response of God – conferring the Holy Spirit.[31]

In subsequent cases throughout the book of Acts all the elements may appear but their order varies. Close scrutiny

---

[28] Geoffrey W.H. Lampe, *The Seal of the Spirit: A Study in the Doctrine of Baptism and Confirmation in the New Testament and the Fathers* (2nd edition, London: SPCK, 1967), p. xxiv.
[29] Ibid., p. 6. Lampe points out that the Greek aorist tense used by Paul refers to a single specific moment, which he believes to be that of (water) baptism 'or rather of the inward experience of which Baptism is the effective symbol', p. 5.
[30] Ibid., p. 64.
[31] James D.G. Dunn, *Baptism in the Holy Spirit: A Re-examination of the New Testament Teaching on the Gift of the Spirit in Relation to Pentecostalism Today* (London: SCM, 1970), ch. 9.

reveals, moreover, that the indispensable prerequisite for (c) is (a) rather than (b). This is evident from no less than five incidents in Acts. Let us consider them in turn:

1. Acts 2:1-4 relates that the Holy Spirit descended on the apostles (and their companions) assembled in a building in Jerusalem at Pentecost.[32] Their only preparation was faith in the risen Lord and an extended period of prayer (Acts 1:14, compare Luke 24:49, 53). Their only baptism in water appears to have been by John the Baptist in preparation for Jesus' ministry, long before.[33]

2. The taking of the Gospel to Samaria described in Acts 8 has posed the greatest problems of all to those trying to make sense of Christian initiation in Acts. The Samaritans are said to have believed Philip preaching about 'the kingdom of God and the name of Jesus Christ' and to have been baptised 'in the name of the Lord Jesus' (vv. 12,16), yet they evidently failed to receive the Holy Spirit until the apostles Peter and John came down from Jerusalem, prayed for them, and laid their hands upon them (vv. 15,17). Why the delay? There have been various explanations:

i) The influential view of Lampe is that the preaching of the Gospel in Samaria was a crucial moment in the advance of the Christian faith (in this case to a people traditionally estranged from the Jews) and needed leaders from Jerusalem to come down and, by a special sign of fellowship, incorporate Samaritan believers into the apostolic Church – the result being a 'Samaritan Pentecost'.[34] But the focus of this passage is not on the pariah status of the Samaritans, but rather on the misdemeanours of Simon the magician.[35]

---

[32] Acts 1:15 speaks of a company of about 120 in all. Dunn thinks almost certainly this larger number is referred to in 2:1 (*Baptism in the Holy Spirit*, p. 40)
[33] Lampe, *Seal of the Spirit*, p. 46, G.R. Beasley-Murray, *Baptism in the New Testament* (London: Macmillan, 1962), pp. 96-8. See Matthew 3:11, Luke 3:16, though John 3:22-24, 4:1 at least allow the possibility that Jesus had himself rebaptised them, but, if so, long before this Pentecost.
[34] Lampe, *Seal of the Spirit*, p. 72.
[35] See James D.G. Dunn, 'They Believed Philip Preaching (Acts 8:12)', *Irish Biblical Studies* 1 (1979), reprinted in James D.G. Dunn, *The Christ and the Spirit*, vol.2 *Pneumatology* (Edinburgh: T. & T. Clark, 1998), p. 219.

ii) G.R. Beasley-Murray suggests that in fact the Samaritan converts had received the Holy Spirit but not the *charismata,* though he does so tentatively to make sense of 'an otherwise incomprehensible situation'.[36] But this is to stand the rest of the evidence of Acts on its head for it is outward phenomena that elsewhere indicate the reception of the Spirit.[37] Their absence indicates the Spirit's absence.

iii) More impressive is Dunn's own observation that the Samaritans' original 'conversion' was in some way defective.[38] The Samaritans were clearly impressed by the miracles performed by Philip but perhaps not drawn to heartfelt repentance. This was certainly the case with Simon the magician who is also described as 'believing' and being baptised (vv. 13, 18-24). We can imagine that Peter and John not only prayed for these Samaritans but also gave some further explanation of the Gospel, which led to first the deepening of their faith-repentance and then reception of the Holy Spirit through the laying on of hands. It may well be that, earlier, superstition or indeed the taint of the occult restricted them, for they had been in great awe of Simon (vv. 9-11).

3. The apostle Paul's case is described in Acts 9. From being a militant opponent of the Christian 'Way' he encountered the risen Christ on the Damascus road, which caused him huge trauma, physical and spiritual. For three days he was blind and neither ate nor drank. No doubt this was a period of profound repentance (*metanoia,* literally 'change of mind', in biblical Greek influenced by the Hebrew *shūv,* 'to turn (around)'). He had been zealous but misguided, but now that he had become a believer in Christ, his whole perspective had changed (Philippians 3:4-11), and he was repentant for all the pain and grief caused formerly

[36] Beasley-Murray, *Baptism in the New Testament,* p. 119.
[37] Wind, fire and tongues (2:2-4), tongues and prophecy (19:6), like the first Christian Pentecost (11:15). See Dunn, *Pneumatology,* p. 217.
[38] Dunn, *Baptism in the Holy Spirit,* p. 65, Dunn, *Pneumatology,* p. 220. He sees an indication of this in the fact that in v. 12 *pisteuein* is followed by the dative – a construction normally meaning in the New Testament 'to believe *about*', 'to believe *that*' – not the common term for conversion *pisteuein eis* 'to believe *in*' (i.e. 'to be committed to').

to Christians (1 Corinthians 15:9). With the laying on of Ananias' hands he then could receive not only physical healing, but also, it seems clear, the Holy Spirit. Baptism followed afterwards (Acts 9:17-19).

4. Acts 10 relates the conversion of Cornelius, the Gentile centurion of the Italian Cohort, and those with him, following the preaching of Peter. It was another immense step in the progress of the Gospel. Peter, a loyal Jew, needed a preparatory vision to convince him of the rightness of entering a Gentile home and evangelising. Once there he spoke about the ministry of Jesus, his death and resurrection, his forthcoming role as judge of all, and the way to forgiveness of sins through faith in him. Before any mention of baptism, the Holy Spirit descended upon his audience in a way clearly resembling the apostles' experience at Pentecost (Acts 11:15, 15:9). It is surely evident that these Gentiles responded to hearing the Gospel with repentance and faith, their hearts being ready then to receive the Spirit without delay.[39] How could Peter withhold baptism? He felt helpless, it seems, before a sovereign act of God (Acts 11:17). Here was another divinely underwritten step in the Church's mission to the Gentile world.

5. The matter of Apollos described in Acts 18 is of considerably less significance yet nonetheless surprising. At Ephesus Priscilla and Aquila, formerly companions of Paul at Corinth, encountered this eloquent Alexandrian Jew. He had received only the baptism of John, yet had clearly received some instruction about Jesus and is described as 'fervent (literally 'boiling') in the Spirit' (v.25).[40] Priscilla and Aquila are said to have given him further Christian instruction but we hear of no further baptism. Beasley-Murray deduces, 'where submission to the Messiah Jesus is accompanied by the possession of the Spirit, Johannine

---

[39] Dunn, *Baptism in the Holy Spirit*, p. 82.

[40] Greek *tō pneumati*. The definite article *tō* here probably points to the Holy Spirit rather than Apollos' own feelings or personality, see F.F. Bruce, *The Acts of the Apostles: the Greek Text with Introduction and Commentary* (3rd edition, Grand Rapids: Eerdmans, 1990), p. 402.

baptism needs no supplementing.'[41] In the incident that follows, Paul encounters disciples baptised by John who were clearly not 'boiling in the Spirit' (Acts 19:1-7). They needed further instruction, rebaptism 'in the name of the Lord Jesus' and the apostle's laying on of hands before they received the Spirit.

This catalogue of special cases reveals clearly that the Spirit is not tied to the administration of sacraments. He 'blows where he wills' (John 3:8) and it is evident he wills to fill truly responsive human hearts. Nonetheless the fact that, in cases 3 and 4, when the converts have received the Spirit independently of water baptism, baptism is afterwards immediately administered, shows that ideally the three elements of 'conversion-initiation' (faith, water baptism and the Holy Spirit) should always be held together. Indeed, bearing in mind Acts 2:38, 1 Corinthians 12:13 and John 3:5 it may be fair to say with Beasley-Murray that, generally in the New Testament, 'baptism is the supreme moment of the impartation of the Spirit...*in the believer*'.[42] But an infant when baptised is not a believer and therefore can scarcely be expected to receive the Spirit in the same way; lacking this, infant baptism is not complete Christian initiation.

Metaphors for Baptism

The New Testament contains a rich array of metaphors for Christian baptism, each of which expresses some aspect of the significance of becoming a Christian.

a) Baptism into the death, burial and resurrection of Christ aptly articulates water baptism by immersion. Paul's use of the metaphor is commonly quoted from Romans 6:3-4. He is driving home the point that a Christian must view his old sinful life as dead, not only drowned but crucified with Christ, so that he may live for God (vv. 6, 10-11). Rising from the water also prefigures ultimate rising from physical

---

[41] Beasley-Murray, *Baptism in the New Testament*, p. 112. See Lampe, *Seal of the Spirit*, p. 66.
[42] Beasley-Murray, *Baptism in the New Testament*, p. 275.

death (v. 5). In the less quoted reiteration of the metaphor in Colossians 2:12 the need for faith in the resurrection of Christ is explicitly stated.

b) 'Putting on' Christ as if clothing at baptism is another attractive metaphor and is seen as a means of obliterating differences of race, class or sex before God (Galatians 3:27-28). The context shows that Paul is applying this metaphor to all who are children of God through faith in Christ Jesus (vv. 23-26). Elsewhere he specifies some of the qualities of character he expects Christians consciously to wear (Colossians 3:12-14).

c) 'Sealing (Greek *sphragizō*) with the Spirit', Lampe tells us, bears its primary religious significance of 'to set a mark of ownership upon', 'to stamp as the personal property (of God)'.[43] Its secular antecedents included tattooing slaves with their owner's name or mark, and marking or tattooing devotees of pagan cults. Within Judaism circumcision fulfilled a similar function (Genesis 17:11) and later the wearing of phylacteries (Deuteronomy 6:8, 11:18). The idea that the 'good' should be marked to distinguish them from the bad and save them from judgement (Ezekiel 9:4-6) proved popular with the writer of the book of Revelation (Revelation 7:3, 9:4). 'Sealing' Christians is applied variously in the Patristic writings to baptism, anointing, laying on of hands, but especially to marking the sign of the cross on neophytes. The three Pauline texts which mention 'sealing', refer to the gift of the Spirit not baptism. Ephesians 1:13 declares that it is those who have heard the Gospel and believed in Christ who are 'sealed with the promised Holy Spirit'.

d) It is widely accepted today that being 'born again' of 'water and the Spirit' (John 3:3, 5) refers specifically to the outward and inward aspects of becoming a Christian.[44] Jesus' statement about the need for new birth to enter the kingdom of God is addressed to the furtive figure of

[43] Lampe, *Seal of the Spirit*, pp. 5ff.
[44] For example, Beasley-Murray, *Baptism in the New Testament*, p. 228.

Nicodemus who, coming to Jesus by night, is clearly in need of the fullness of faith. In 1 Peter 1:23-25 the same metaphor is used explicitly of those responding to the Gospel.

e) The passage likening baptism to the flood waters of the time of Noah (1 Peter 3:20-22) is rather obscure. It speaks of water as being in both cases the medium through which people obtain salvation. The baptismal water's effectiveness is said to be through its association with the resurrection of Jesus Christ (compare Romans 6:4). In the context is a reference to Christ's death for our sins (v. 18). And does the Greek phrase *eperotema* (*eis theon*) (v. 21), translated variously 'appeal', 'pledge' or 'promise' (to God), but which could also mean 'question' or 'enquiry' (into God), convey a hint of the solemn questions put to the candidates for baptism? No certainty is possible,[45] but that believers are in mind is shown by the earlier reference to new birth through hearing the Christian Gospel proclaimed (1:23-25).

These vivid and varied metaphors and images, then, which so helpfully amplify our understanding of the sacrament, are in fact all speaking of the baptism of believers. Lampe himself acknowledges this when he says:

> 'Despite various possible indications of the existence of infant Baptism in the New Testament, the theology of Baptism therein presented to us is concerned with the Baptism of adults alone.'[46]

One cannot then simply apply such metaphors to the baptism of infants, who are quite unconscious of what is happening, as the compilers of the Church of England's liturgical manual *Common Worship*, appear intent on doing in their prayer over the baptismal water (making no distinction between infants and believing candidates):

> 'We thank you, Father, for the water of baptism. In it we are buried with Christ in his death. By it we share in his resurrection. Through it we are reborn by the Holy Spirit.'

---

[45] See C.E.B. Cranfield, *1 and 2 Peter and Jude* (London: SCM, 1960), p. 106f.

[46] Lampe, *Seal of the Spirit*, p. 93. See Beasley-Murray, *Baptism in the New Testament*, p. 274.

Then, perhaps with some stirring of biblical awareness, they continue:

> 'Therefore, in joyful obedience to your Son, we baptise into his fellowship those who come to him *in faith.*'

If indeed infant baptism was practised in New Testament times, practice ran ahead of theology. If filling with the Spirit requires the faith-repentance of the candidate then, in general, with infants it awaits a later time. The value of Anglican confirmation since the Reformation is that it has, for candidates who have reached the 'years of discretion' or beyond, afforded just such an occasion. But this depends on careful instruction that may bring them to a point of faith-repentance and commitment. Confirmation, without this, is no more effective in preparing its candidates for being filled with the Holy Spirit than infant baptism. That filling will then await an occasion or series of occasions outside the sacramental system of the Church when God brings those candidates to an awareness of their need and of his love and forgiveness, and they respond.[47]

The Laying on of Hands

Water refreshing dry ground may be a good analogy for God's Spirit invigorating the human soul (Isaiah 44:3), but this is not the import of water in baptism. Applied only externally to the candidate, it signifies the washing away of sin[48] or (in immersion) death of the old self-centred nature, but scarcely suggests filling with the Spirit. Oscar Cullmann then, was surely right to see this as a reason for the development of other rites within what became an initiation complex – particularly the laying on of hands and anointing.[49]

---

[47] Whilst recognising the reality of God's grace, Beasley-Murray is surely right when he says, 'The human element in faith cannot be eliminated nor man's responsibility for his decision denied' (*Baptism in the New Testament*, p. 271).
[48] See the Prayer Book baptismal service: 'Almighty and everlasting God, who of thy great mercy ... didst sanctify water to the mystical washing away of sin ...'
[49] Oscar Cullmann, 'La Signification du Baptême dans le Nouveau Testament', *Revue de Théologie et de Philosophie* 30 (1942), pp. 121-34.

In the New Testament the laying on of hands by apostles is found, as we have mentioned above, in the case of the Samaritans (Acts 8:14-17) and the Ephesian 'brethren' (Acts 19:6).[50] In the first case this may have been an emergency procedure for those who, unexpectedly it seems (in the light of 2:38), had clearly not been filled with the Holy Spirit at the time of their baptism. But, whereas this incident took place in the first year or so of the Church's life, the second occurred more than 20 years later. Colin Buchanan regards it as another 'emergency' in the life of the Church requiring special action.[51] Lampe sees it as 'another decisive moment in the missionary history', Ephesus being the next centre of the Gentile mission after Antioch, the first converts there needing to be incorporated into the Church with a special sign of apostolic welcome.[52] But Luke's narrative makes no special issue of it, simply mentioning that Paul laid hands on these converts immediately after baptising them in the name of the Lord Jesus. In the twenty years since the first evangelising of Samaria, baptismal practice may have begun to develop into a more complex rite including (sometimes at least) the laying on of hands. Paul may have been influenced here by the fact that he had himself received the Holy Spirit through this means (Acts 9:17). We cannot be certain. Paul is not recorded as laying hands on Lydia and her household (Acts 16:15), the Philippian jailer and his household (16:31-4), or the Corinthian converts (18:8), but Luke does not give us a full account of each initiation scene. Surely Lydia, the jailer and the Corinthians received the Spirit when they were baptised, but even this is not mentioned. The laying on of hands may then have been a more common feature of early Christian initiation than is specifically indicated by Luke.[53]

[50] F.F. Bruce suggests there may have been an intentional parallel between the two events, as in Acts there are often counterparts by Paul of earlier activities by Peter; Bruce, *Acts* (London: Marshall, Morgan & Scott, 1954), p. 386.
[51] Buchanan, *Anglican Confirmation*, p. 9.
[52] Lampe, *Seal of the Spirit*, p. 76.
[53] Compare Beasley-Murray, *Baptism in the New Testament*, p. 123: 'It cannot be assumed that the Samaritans were the only people on whom Peter and John laid hands that they might receive the blessing of the Spirit and it is similarly conceivable that Paul sometimes used the rite in administering baptism.'

Where he mentions initiation at all he refers to the central feature, (water) baptism.

This might explain why the Epistle to the Hebrews, written it seems before AD 70 by a convert of the apostles (Hebrews 2:3), from Rome or Ephesus,[54] implies laying on of hands is by then a regular part of the initiation procedure. The author writes:

> 'Let us leave the elementary doctrines of Christ and go on to maturity, not laying again a foundation of repentance from dead works and of faith toward God, with instruction about ablutions, the laying on of hands, the resurrection of the dead, and eternal judgement.' (6:1-2)

The author is clearly describing early doctrinal instruction and practice in the Church he knew. Hugh Montefiore, whether or not he is right in championing Apollos as the author, may be right in seeing the use of *baptismos* (not the normal word in the New Testament for baptism, though so used by Josephus) in the plural here as a reflection of the double baptism some had received: that of John the Baptist (and disciples) and that in the name of the Lord Jesus.[55] But he is surely wrong to think the laying on of hands referred to here is an 'emergency procedure' for those who have undergone the two rites. It appears rather as regular a part of the instruction as the resurrection of the dead and eternal judgement.

A further confirmation of the more general use of the laying on of hands is found in 2 Timothy 1:6. Paul is encouraging Timothy to rekindle 'the gift'[56] received through the laying on of his hands, a spirit (Spirit) of power, love and

[54] F.F. Bruce, *Hebrews* (London: Marshall, Morgan & Scott, 1964), p. 415; Hugh Montefiore, *Hebrews* (London: A. & C. Black, 1964), p. 28.
[55] Montefiore, *Hebrews*, p. 106. C.K. Barrett, *1 Corinthians* (London: A. & C. Black, 1968), p. 10 is not moved by Montefiore's case for Apollos as author. Early writers attributed the epistle to several other authors.
[56] The Greek word here is *charisma* whereas in Acts 2:38 it is *dorea*. However, in Ephesians 4:7-8, speaking of Christ's gifts to the Church, Paul uses *dorea* and *doma*. Clearly there was some interchangeability of these words – as found in the Patristic writings.

self-control. Even Buchanan is prepared to admit this *could just* be post-baptismal and initiatory![57]

From where did the laying on of hands in the Early Church originate? Beasley-Murray quotes from David Daube, who distinguishes between occasions in the Old Testament when people *leant* (Hebrew *samach*) on others or on animals and 'poured' their personality into them (as on sacrificial animals (e.g. Leviticus 1:4) or at the consecration of Levites (Numbers 8:10)), and occasions of simply *placing* hands (Hebrew *sim* or *shith*) on others in blessing (e.g. Genesis 48:14). Moses 'leant' on Joshua, preparing him as his successor (Numbers 27:18-23, Deuteronomy 34:9), and Daube is convinced Christian initiatory laying on of hands likewise falls under the first category. But Beasley-Murray thinks the latter.[58] Is not Daube right here? As God's Spirit was 'poured' into Joshua, so God's Spirit was 'poured' into new members of the Church. For Lampe then to see the laying on of hands in Acts 8:17, 9:17, and 19:6 as merely 'a sign of association in the apostolic or missionary task of the Church' is to rob it of its potency.[59] Such a sign of association rather was 'the right hand of fellowship' given by the 'pillars' of the Church, James, Peter and John, to Paul and Barnabas for their Gentile mission (Galatians 2:9). And for Lampe to describe the laying on of hands after baptism referred to in Hebrews 6:2 as 'almost corresponding to the handshake with which a new member would be received by the president of a modern society' is quite laughable.[60]

How far the laying on of hands in initiation continued to be associated with the conferring of the Holy Spirit on baptised believers is a matter for the next chapter of this book. Before leaving the New Testament, however, we must now look at an important piece of Pauline teaching about the other gospel sacrament.

---

[57] Buchanan, *Anglican Confirmation*, p. 11.
[58] Beasley-Murray, *Baptism in the New Testament*, pp. 122ff.
[59] Lampe, *Seal of the Spirit*, p. 76.
[60] Ibid., p. 78.

Discerning the Lord's Body

Matters relating to the Lord's Supper are found in 1 Corinthians 10 – 11. In chapter 10 St Paul takes up again the matter of food offered to idols (his previous discussion was in chapter 8). In verses 1-10 in somewhat enigmatic fashion he speaks of the people of Israel, in their wilderness wanderings, as privileged with baptism of a sort, 'spiritual food' (manna – Exodus 16) and 'spiritual drink' (water from the rock struck by Moses – Exodus 17), and yet not being protected from God's punishment when they acted in a disobedient and reckless fashion. And he uses this to warn the Corinthian Christians that, baptised participants of the body and blood of Christ though they may be, they yet risk provoking God's jealous anger by eating food offered to idols and so linking themselves with demons (vv. 20-22)

Glenn Davies makes much of the fact that Paul repeatedly declares that *all* the Israelites were baptised, ate and drank, claiming that this must include *children*.[61] As then children participated in these 'sacraments' of the Old Covenant they must be eligible for those of the New. But how significant really is the repeated 'all'? It is merely emphasising that the disobedient, reckless ones were included amongst those who had partaken of the 'spiritual' fare (that 'provided by the Spirit of God'[62]) and yet were punished. That there were children present probably never even entered the apostle's mind.

1 Corinthians 11 is of far greater relevance to our discussion. It contains probably the earliest account of the institution of the Lord's Supper (AD 55, from Ephesus), independent of the written gospels yet confirming to quite a large extent the tradition they embody. It is recounted in the context of a life situation within an apostolic church. Establishing the exact words used by Christ is not the remit of our present examination. But, as the Last Supper took

---

[61] Davies, 'The Lord's Supper for the Lord's Children', pp. 13-16.

[62] A.C. Thiselton, *1 Corinthians: A Commentary on the Greek Text* (Grand Rapids: Eerdmans, 2000), p. 726.

place the night before Jesus was crucified, it might be expected that when the bread and the wine were identified with the body and the (new covenant) blood of Christ this bore some relationship to the horrifying ordeal then imminent. St Paul's first comment, after giving us the words of Christ, explicitly confirms this: 'For as often as you eat this bread and drink the cup, you proclaim the Lord's death until he comes' (v. 26).

The passage that follows warns of the consequences of partaking of the bread and the cup without keeping Christ's death firmly in mind. A person doing so will be held guilty of (profaning) the Lord's broken body and shed blood (v. 27). Rather, he should 'conduct a rigorous self-examination' (v. 28).[63] For him to partake without 'discerning (*diakrin_n*) the body of the Lord' draws (God's) judgement upon himself (v. 29). There are those who would see in v.29, in the use of the word 'body' without 'blood', a reference not to the sacramental bread but to the church.[64] But whilst the metaphor of 'body' for the church is indeed mentioned in 10:17 it is not explained until 12:12-30. 11:29, read straightforwardly, is surely merely recapping and developing a little further v.27, leaving out 'and blood' no doubt to avoid being pedantic. It is most unlikely that Paul would, into the midst of this focused passage, without explanation, introduce a different meaning of 'body'.[65]

We may surely conclude then that, as infants and small children can neither rigorously examine themselves nor discern the significance of the sacramental bread and wine, it is better that they should not communicate but rather wait

[63] Leon Morris, *1 Corinthians* (London: Tyndale, 1958), p. 163, drawing out the implications of *dokimazein* 'to test' (as of assaying metals).

[64] For example, Gordon Fee, *1 Corinthians* (Grand Rapids: Eerdmans, 1987), p. 563; Buchanan, *Children in Communion*, p. 11.

[65] See Thiselton, *1 Corinthians*, pp. 891-4 for a full discussion of this text. He points out that the lexical meaning of *diakrinein* is 'to separate, to make a distinction, to differentiate' and refers to C.K. Barrett's remark that interpreting 'body' here as 'church' would strain the meaning of the Greek. It is worth noting too that Paul refers here to 'the body *of the Lord*' as in v. 27, whereas in 10:17 where 'body' is indubitably used of the church this phrase is absent.

until the 'years of discretion' (at least 12) for this privilege.[66] Against this view so long maintained by the reformed Churches it is now asserted that, as this passage relates to a specific situation in the life of the Corinthian church, and refers to miscreant *adult* behaviour, it should not be developed into a general rule, particularly one debarring small children from communion.[67] In response it is fair to point out that *most* of the New Testament epistles were written to address particular problems faced by first-century churches, yet that has not prevented the Church in all ages from applying their teaching far more generally. The point at issue here is unreflective, unworthy participation in communion. If children, because of the elementary stage of their mental and spiritual development are not aware of what is going on, they may well act inappropriately – anecdotal evidence tells of small children sometimes spitting out the consecrated elements and older ones larking about and even re-entering the communion queue to obtain a 'second snack'! Diligent parents are no doubt scandalised by the thought of such behaviour, but not all children in our age are well instructed or under good control. A rule then derived from this passage restricting the sacrament to those who are older and better able to understand the significance of Christ crucified and risen, and therefore participating reverently, is surely a valuable preventative measure. To include the small children by giving them a blessing, blessed common bread (as in the later Medieval Church[68]), or perhaps a sweetened 'agape wafer' is important.

---

[66] The term 'years of discretion' can be traced back as far as the Fourth Lateran Council (1215). The actual age subsequently varied between ten and fourteen. See J.D.C. Fisher, *Christian Initiation: The Reformation Period*, Alcuin Club Collections 51 (London: SPCK, 1970), p. 238f; Dalby, *Infant Communion*, pp. 21-6.

[67] Committee on Paedocommunion, 1988 Majority Report to the General Assembly of the Orthodox Presbyterian Church, pp. 11,15; Davies, 'The Lord's Supper for the Lord's Children', pp. 18-19.

[68] See Dalby, *Infant Communion*, p. 22.

Conclusions

We may summarise the main thrust of the above argumentation in four points:

1. If the New Testament generally associates the gift of the Holy Spirit with baptism, it is with the baptism of those who have repented and put their faith in Jesus Christ. Infants lacked this and their initiation was therefore incomplete.

2. The rich array of metaphors employed in the New Testament to describe baptism are referring to those who have faith, and cannot be straightforwardly applied to the baptism of infants.

3. The laying on of hands by someone already filled with God's Spirit is a more appropriate sign of conferring the Spirit than washing with water, and may well have come into much more widespread use in New Testament times than is commonly thought.

4. To receive the body and blood of Christ worthily in the communion one needs to be old enough to discern the significance of the consecrated bread and wine. It makes sense then that this should follow a sincere profession of faith in Christ, reception of God's Spirit, and full sacramental initiation into the Church.

CHAPTER FOUR
THE EARLY CHURCH

Having looked at the New Testament for information about Christian initiation and related matters in the earliest decades of the life of the Church, we now move on to consider the situation in subsequent centuries.

Lampe declares that from the New Testament period to the late second century there is no explicit evidence that there existed any initiatory ceremonies besides baptism in water.[69] Subsequently New Testament simplicity was lost and the theology of initiation became confused amidst a complex of rites.[70] How far is this a fair assessment? We shall consider key writers from the second and third centuries, and then look briefly at the wider scene before drawing conclusions.

The Second Century

The Epistle of Barnabas

The *Epistle of Barnabas* is the work of a Jewish Christian (not the Barnabas of the New Testament) and probably dates from AD 120–130. Quoting from 11.1 Lampe translates: 'we go down (into the baptismal water) laden with sins and filth', we rise from it 'bearing fruit in the heart, having fear and hope in Jesus in the Spirit'.[71] That those baptised received a divine indwelling presence is confirmed in 16.8 where the author declares:

> Having received forgiveness of our sins and put our hope in the Name (of the Lord) we were made new, recreated from the beginning. Therefore in our abode truly God dwells in us.

[69] Lampe, *Seal of the Spirit*, p. xix and frequently thereafter.
[70] Ibid., ch. 7.
[71] Ibid., p. 104.

But clearly God's Spirit is granted to a *believer* for he continues, 'How so? Why (by) his word of *faith*, his call of promise...' That faith is a crucial prerequisite is shown again in an earlier passage (6.17) where he simply says, without even mentioning baptism, 'after we have entered into life through *belief* in the promise and through the word...', speaking of the step of becoming a Christian.

Justin

From the middle of the second century we have the well-known account of Christian baptism by the converted philosopher Justin Martyr in his *First Apology*, addressed to the Roman emperor Antoninus Pius. He says:

> As many as are persuaded and believe that what we teach and say is true, and undertake to be able to live accordingly, are instructed to pray and to entreat God with fasting, for the remission of their sins that are past, we praying and fasting with them. Then they are brought by us where there is water, and are regenerated in the same manner in which we were ourselves regenerated. For, in the name of God, the Father and Lord of the universe, and of our Saviour Jesus Christ, and of the Holy Spirit, they then receive the washing with water.[72]

A little later he tells us that this step is also called 'illumination' because those baptised are illuminated in understanding by what they learn.

Lampe is right, we have no indication here of any initiatory rite other than baptism in water, through which the candidates are brought cleansing and new birth. This may well be, however, because this is an abbreviated account for pagan readers and, for that reason, it omits any reference to subsidiary rites. It does not even mention that the candidates received the Holy Spirit. Even so, it shows that water baptism[73] in the three-fold Name was the central feature of Christian initiation. Its association with the Holy Spirit is implied elsewhere when Justin asks in dialogue with Trypho the Jew, 'What need have I of that other

---

[72] Justin, 1 *Apology* 61, Ante-Nicene Fathers edition [ANF].
[73] Elsewhere Justin refers to it as 'the water of life' (*Dialogue with Trypho* 14.1).

baptism [i.e. circumcision] who have been baptised with the Holy Spirit?'[74] And he goes on to state that daily those becoming Christians 'are also receiving gifts, each as he is worthy, illuminated through the name of this Christ', such gifts as foreknowledge and healing[75] – surely a reference to some of the gifts of the Spirit in 1 Corinthians 12. But clearly from 1 *Apology* 61 the range of spiritual blessings that flow from baptism is bestowed on those who repent, believe, and commit themselves to the cause of Christ.

Irenaeus

In contrast to much thinking today Irenaeus, bishop of Lyons in the latter part of the second century, saw no dichotomy between the institution of the Church on the one hand, and the work of the Holy Spirit on the other. He firmly believed the Spirit was at the very heart of the life of the Church:

> For where the Church is there is the Spirit of God, and where the Spirit of God is there is the Church, and every kind of grace; but the Spirit is truth.[76]

And the Spirit is given to the believer at baptism. Commenting on St Paul's words in 1 Corinthians 15:49 and 6:11 he asks:

> When (do we bear) the image of the heavenly (Adam)? Doubtless when he says, "You have been washed, believing in the name of the Lord, and receiving his Spirit." [77]

Elsewhere he tells us baptism is administered in the three-fold Name and 'is the seal of eternal life, and is the new birth unto God.'[78] Somewhat surprisingly, in *Against Heresies* 4.38.2, he interprets 1 Corinthians 3:2 ('I fed you with milk not solid food') as meaning that the Corinthians had merely heard about the human Jesus but had not yet received the Spirit, and he continues, 'the apostle had the

---

[74] Justin, *Dialogue with Trypho* 29.1.
[75] Justin, *Dialogue with Trypho* 39.2.
[76] Irenaeus, *Against Heresies* 3.24.1.
[77] Irenaeus, *Against Heresies* 5.11.2. See also Irenaeus, *Demonstration of the Apostolic Preaching* 42.
[78] Irenaeus, *Demonstration of the Apostolic Preaching* 3.

power to give them solid food – for those upon whom the apostles laid hands received the Holy Spirit, who is the food of life (eternal) – but they were not capable of receiving it.' Lampe comments ruefully, 'Here is the first clear instance of the impact of Acts 8:17 on the Patristic theology of Baptism.'[79] But he rightly observes that Irenaeus gives no indication that this relates to contemporary practice.

Before leaving Irenaeus it is important to note that he, like 'Barnabas' and Justin, speaks of the Spirit's being conferred on baptised *believers*.

Early Gnosticism

When rites other than water baptism did appear in the Church's regular initiatory practices *the laying on of hands* could, as we have seen in the previous chapter, claim New Testament precedent, but not so the use of *oil*.[80] In contrast, the use of oil by some of the Gnostic sects is well attested.[81] Denying Christ's true incarnation and the reality of the atonement, Lampe suggests, made water baptism of limited value to the Gnostics.[82] Other, more exotic rites, derived perhaps from the pagan mystery religions, replaced or supplemented it, most notably the use of oil (chrism). A rationale is spelt out in the so-called *Gospel of Philip*:

> The chrism is superior to baptism, for it is from the word 'chrism' that we have been called 'Christians', certainly not from the word 'baptism'.[83]

It has been suggested that initiatory unction (chrismation) made its way into orthodox Christian circles

[79] Lampe, *Seal of the Spirit*, p. 118.
[80] Unless perhaps baptismal chrism derived ultimately from anointing with oil for healing (James 5:14). In the mildly Gnostic *Acts of Thomas* 121, 157 (Syriac) physical healing is one of the blessings expected from the oil used in initiation. Furthermore, whilst in Hippolytus' *Apostolic Tradition* 5 the prayer over the oil offered for *healing* recalls that oil was used for anointing kings, priests and prophets, Tertullian derives *baptismal* anointing from the anointing of priests (*On Baptism* 7).
[81] For example, the Marcosians (Irenaeus, *Against Heresies* 1.21.4), the Naassenes (Hippolytus, *Heresies* 5.2), the Orphites (Origen, *Against Celsus* 6.27-8), and the Marcionites (Tertullian, *Against Marcion* 1.14).
[82] Lampe, *Seal of the Spirit*, p. 121.
[83] Logion 95.

from Gnosticism, assisted by the relative fluidity of doctrine and practice in the second century.[84] However, this derivation is not certain. Gregory Dix would deny such an idea, and Lampe himself concedes that unction, like signing the initiate with the cross, would probably have developed anyway from Scriptural metaphors.[85]

The Third Century and Beyond

From the beginning of the third century Christian initiation appears at once as a *complex* of rites, though their nature and order are not uniform throughout the Church. We shall study the evidence of four authors in some detail and then look briefly at the wider scene.

Tertullian

Tertullian, the eloquent North African apologist for the Christian faith, whose many writings come from the end of the second and the first two decades of the third century, affords us considerable insight into the constituent elements of the baptismal procedure he knew.[86] Information comes principally from his work *On Baptism,* but there are also references scattered through his other writings.[87] The elements are:

renunciation of 'the devil, his pomp and his angels'

confession of faith

immersion in water three times (in the name of the persons of the Trinity)

anointing with oil (chrism)

signing with the cross

laying on of (the president's) hands.

---

[84] Lampe, *Seal of the Spirit,* pp. 127-31; Klaus Thraede, 'Exorzismus', *Reallexikon für Antike und Christentum,* vol. 7 (Stuttgart, 1969), p. 85.
[85] *The Treatise on the Apostolic Tradition of St Hippolytus of Rome* edited by Gregory Dix (1937, reissued London: SPCK, 1968), p. xxxix; Lampe, *Seal of the Spirit,* p. 130.
[86] The North African Church clearly had a close relationship with the Church in Rome, so we should expect some kinship between the practice of the two churches.
[87] See Tertullian, *On Shows* 4, *On Baptism* 6-8, *On the Resurrection of the Flesh* 8, *On Military Crowns* 3.

Those baptised then partook of a mixture of milk and honey, joined in prayers for God's bestowal of the *charismata*, and shared daily before daybreak in the eucharist of the local church.[88] The proper minister of baptism, he says, is the bishop, or presbyters or deacons he authorises; even a layman may baptise in emergency.[89] Baptism appears then as a complex event and from it flow a range of spiritual benefits: remission of sins, deliverance from death, new birth, and the bestowal of the Holy Spirit.[90]

But Lampe is far from happy with the North African theologian. He accuses him of inconsistency for using the term 'baptism' both of immersion in water[91] and as an umbrella term for the whole complex rite of initiation;[92] also for speaking of the Holy Spirit as bringing people to new birth through the water[93] yet maintaining the Spirit was actually conferred through the later rite of the laying on of the president's hand.[94] Lampe concludes:

> We must hold his confused thought on Baptism and the laying on of hands responsible in no small measure for the difficulties and ambiguities which have continued from his days to our own to hamper the working out of a reasoned theology of the operation of the Holy Spirit in Baptism and Confirmation.[95]

It is not surprising that Lampe wishes to discredit Tertullian, for the North African is one of the principal witnesses called by his adversaries A.J. Mason and Dix;[96] but, in fact, his accusations do not score heavily. Tertullian's use of 'baptism' as an umbrella term tells us two things: (i) he regards the whole initiation complex as essentially one entity, and (ii) the water rite is its central element.

---

[88] Tertullian, *On Military Crowns* 3, *On Baptism* 20.
[89] Tertullian, *On Baptism* 17.
[90] Tertullian, *Against Marcion* 1.28.
[91] Tertullian, *On Prescription against Heretics* 36.
[92] In the title *On Baptism*.
[93] Tertullian, *On the Soul* 41.
[94] Tertullian, *On Baptism* 8, *On the Resurrection of the Flesh* 8.
[95] Lampe, *Seal of the Spirit*, p. 162.
[96] A.J. Mason, *The Relation of Confirmation to Baptism, as Taught in Holy Scripture and the Fathers* (London: Longmans, 1891), pp. 59ff; Gregory Dix, *The Theology of Confirmation in Relation to Baptism* (London: Dacre, 1946), p. 14.

His use of the term 'baptism' in this way surely leaves open the possibility that earlier writers may, at least sometimes, have done the same. Regarding Lampe's criticisms, Tertullian's analytical mind likes to allocate different spiritual blessings to different parts of the initiation sequence and sees in the laying on of the president's hand the moment when the Holy Spirit is bestowed on the candidate. But he believes the Spirit is involved to a degree in the other parts of the sequence too. When he speaks of the soul's renewal 'in its second birth by water and the power from on high', his phraseology is no doubt influenced by John 3:5.[97] Connecting the water with new birth is almost axiomatic amongst the Fathers, regardless of when they see the Holy Spirit actually conferred.

Lampe thinks Tertullian, in linking the Holy Spirit with the laying on of hands, in all probability betrays the recent influence of the Book of Acts upon the North African Church. But this is by no means established. The fact that Tertullian does not appeal to Acts at all to justify this practice only makes more probable a different explanation, as Lampe grudgingly concedes: Tertullian in this matter may be following ancient tradition within the Church (perhaps reflected in Hebrews 6:2).[98]

It is clear too that Tertullian believes that, for baptism to be effective, a candidate needs true faith. Commenting on John the Baptist's declaration that the coming One would baptise with Spirit and fire he says:

> because a true and steadfast faith is baptised with (the Spirit)[99] unto salvation; but a feigned and feeble faith is baptised with fire unto judgement.

This is one of the main reasons Tertullian prefers the baptism of little children to be delayed. Commenting on a

---

[97] Tertullian, *On the Soul* 41. See also Tertullian, *On Baptism* 13

[98] Lampe, *Seal of the Spirit*, p. 161. Alistair Stewart-Sykes' recent erudite study, 'Manumission and Baptism in Tertullian's Africa', *Studia Liturgica* 31 (2001), pp. 129-49, submitting that the laying on of hands in baptism came from the secular ritual of freeing a slave, disregards completely the biblical roots of the practice.

[99] Tertullian, *On Baptism* 10. The translator, Ernest Evans, thinks that 'with water', which is in the Latin here, was a slip of the pen.

text clearly favourable to infant baptism, 'Forbid them not to come to me', he says:

> So let them come, when they are growing up, when they are learning, when they are being taught what they are coming to: let them be made Christians when they have become competent to know Christ...Let them first learn how to ask for salvation.[100]

If baptism should be then delayed, so also necessarily a child's participation in the eucharist which is the entitlement of the baptised.

Hippolytus

Hippolytus was the most important third-century theologian of the Roman Church, of wide interests, to whom many writings are attributed. His *Apostolic Tradition* is of particular importance.[101] Originally written in Greek, it is now preserved in a damaged but literal Latin translation and in various ancient Eastern versions which stem from a common original. It is a 'Church Order', giving a series of instructions about the correct ordering of church life, though its claim to be apostolic is generally rejected today. Rather it is, it seems, Hippolytus' version of the practice of the Roman Church perhaps a little before his time.[102]

The complexity of the baptismal ritual suggests it may have been elaborated somewhat according to later custom by those using and copying it in Oriental churches.[103] Nonetheless its general outline bears considerable similarity to what Tertullian has said about baptism and to later Roman practice.

---

[100] Tertullian, *On Baptism* 18. Tertullian is in fact the first explicit witness to the practice of infant baptism. M.E. Johnson believes his strong protest against it implies its widespread acceptance in North Africa: *The Rites of Christian Initiation: Their Evolution and Interpretation* (Collegeville: Liturgical Press, 1999), p. 65.
[101] Conveniently available in the English translation of G.J. Cuming, *Hippolytus: A Text for Students* (Grove Liturgical Study 8, 2nd edition, 1987).
[102] Lampe, *Seal of the Spirit*, p. 129.
[103] See Paul Bradshaw, *Search for the Origins of Christian Worship: Sources and Methods for the Study of Early Liturgy* (2nd edition, London: SPCK, 2002), ch. 4.

A three-year preparation (catechumenate) is necessary before baptism, and each catechumen must undergo an extended series of exorcisms both before and during the baptismal procedure. After renouncing Satan, his service and all his works the catechumen undergoes a three-fold baptism, each part relating to one person of the Trinity, being questioned about his faith from an interrogative form of something resembling our Apostles' Creed. Then there is a preliminary anointing by a presbyter, after which the bishop lays his hand on each catechumen and prays. Exactly *what* he prays has been the subject of dispute. The Latin translation says:

> 'O Lord God, who has made these worthy to merit remission of sins through the laver (washing) of regeneration of the Holy Spirit, send on them your grace that they may serve you according to your will.'

The Oriental versions, however, have in place of the phrase 'of the Holy Spirit' the words, 'make them worthy to be filled with the Holy Spirit, and', which seems to be pointing to the bishop's anointing them with oil in the three-fold Name, which follows immediately afterwards.

Which represents the original text? Lampe, in the first edition of *The Seal of the Spirit*, argues at length in favour of the normally reliable Latin;[104] Dix regards it as corrupt here and favours the Oriental versions.[105] By the second edition of *The Seal of the Spirit*, Lampe had moderated his position, feeling probably that Hippolytus, like Tertullian, sees the baptismal washing as preliminary to another rite (in this case the anointing by the bishop that follows the prayer) when the Holy Spirit is bestowed.[106] This tallies well with Hippolytus' view expressed elsewhere that the oil with which believers are anointed after the laver is 'the power of the

---

[104] Lampe, *Seal of the Spirit*, pp. 136ff. This view is now strongly upheld by Aidan Kavanagh in his *Confirmation: Origins and Reform* (New York: Pueblo, 1988) p. 47.

[105] Hippolytus, *Apostolic Tradition* p. 38 (Dix edition).

[106] Lampe, *Seal of the Spirit*, p. xvii. Other later scholars have put forward other solutions, including refusing to accord priority to any version, see Anthony Gelston, 'A Note on the Text of the *Apostolic Tradition* of Hippolytus ' & G.J. Cuming, 'The Post-Baptismal Prayer in *Apostolic Tradition*: Further Reflections', *Journal of Theological Studies* 39 (April 1988), pp. 112-9.

Holy Spirit'.[107] In other passages Hippolytus speaks of 'the laver of regeneration which renews the believing'[108] and declares of Jesus' baptism, 'As (he) rose out of the Jordan, he purified the water and bestowed on it the grace of the Holy Spirit.'[109] And so Lampe accuses Hippolytus too of considerable confusion of thought. But Hippolytus, like Tertullian, whilst associating the bestowal of the Holy Spirit with one particular rite, cannot dissociate the Spirit from the rest, in particular the water of new birth.

The *Apostolic Tradition* also refers to the baptism of little children, saying they are to be baptised first and, if they are too young to answer the questions themselves, their parents or another relative may answer for them.[110] Did they, like the adults, go on to partake of the mixture of milk and honey (resembling Israel's entry to the Promised Land) *and* the eucharistic bread and wine? Hippolytus does not tell us.

Origen

Few today would dispute that Origen was the greatest theologian of the eastern patristic church. He was certainly its most prolific writer. His career spanned the first half of the third century, first in Alexandria, then in Caesarea. With regard to baptism Origen's emphasis is on the correct state of heart of the participants and its spiritual effects, not on particular liturgical actions. Having heard the word of God people should root sin out of their lives and come with meekness and humility,[111] then 'what is called the laver of regeneration takes place with renewal of the Spirit'.[112] Baptism does not automatically confer the Holy Spirit. Reflecting on the incidents of Acts 10 and 8, Origen notes that Cornelius was a catechumen who merited receiving the

[107] Hippolytus, *On Daniel* 1.16.3.
[108] Hippolytus, *On Antichrist* 59.
[109] *Drei georgisch erhaltenen Schriften von Hippolytus*, edited by G.N. Bonwetsch, *Texte und Untersuchungen zur Geschichte der altchristlichen Literatur* 11 (Leipzig, 1904), p. 30.
[110] Hippolytus, *Apostolic Tradition* 21.
[111] Origen, *Homilies on Leviticus* 6.2.
[112] Origen, *Commentary on John* 6.17 (ANF).

Holy Spirit before coming to the water, whilst Simon, who had accepted baptism, was refused that gift.[113] Lampe thinks Origen's insistence on the inward and ethical leads him 'to employ some rather confused language' when speaking of the bestowal of the Spirit.[114] But Origen is only faithfully following St Paul (Galatians 3:2). Baptism is administered, says Origen, in the three-fold Name and this confers power on the water.[115] Origen knows of the use of oil in the initiatory procedure but appears not to attach great significance to it. Whilst he recognises too that the Holy Spirit was conferred through the laying on of the apostles' hands, he gives no indication that this is reflected in contemporary Eastern practice.[116]

In several passages Origen testifies to infant baptism as the custom of the Church and he declares the tradition was received from the apostles,[117] though he admits there is much discussion in the church as to whether it is necessary and he quotes as Scriptural justification, 'No-one is pure from stain, even though he be but one day old' (Job 14:4, LXX). How Origen squares infant baptism with his insistence elsewhere on the correct state of the heart, he does not explain.

Origen's *Homilies on Judges* 6.2 contains an intriguing reference to 'little children' who, before they know how to fight the Lord's battles, or can eat the heavenly bread, the flesh of the immaculate Lamb, and drink of the true vine, are supported by the angels. Later, when they are themselves old enough to be heavenly soldiers and are sustained by this nourishment, they can fight for themselves. It may be that Origen is referring here to catechumens, for they are capable of receiving elementary Christian teaching though, just like

[113] Origen, *Homilies on Numbers* 3.1.
[114] Lampe, *Seal of the Spirit*, p. 164.
[115] Origen, *On First Principles* 1.3.2. See Henri Crouzel, *Origen* (Edinburgh: T. & T. Clark, 1989), p. 225.
[116] Lampe, *Seal of the Spirit*, pp. 166ff.
[117] Origen, *Commentary on Romans* 5.9, *Homilies on Leviticus* 8.3. Whilst this is impossible to prove, Johnson accepts that infant baptism must have been a long-standing tradition in the Alexandrian Church (*Rites of Christian Initiation*, p. 59).

little children, they are in the charge of angelic powers.[118] But another possibility is that he is thinking of the children of Christian parents who, baptised in infancy, are only later and after instruction, admitted to the eucharist, for there is in fact no reference in this passage to a forthcoming baptism, which we should expect alluded to as a vital source of spiritual strength for the catechumen.

Cyprian

Cyprian led the Church of North Africa during a very difficult decade in the middle of the third century. In 250 and again in 257-258 there were empire-wide persecutions of the Church during which many lapsed, denying their allegiance to Christ. Following the first persecution the question arose: on what terms could the lapsed be received back into the Church? Fierce disputes and schisms developed within the Church. Then there arose the further question: on what conditions could schismatics and even heretics be admitted to the Church? In such turbulent times baptismal doctrine was tested and developed.

Like Tertullian, Cyprian believed remission of sins and new birth are received in the water of baptism. Lampe exults that Cyprian declares, 'as often as water is named alone in the Holy Scriptures, baptism is referred to' and says that baptism confers the Holy Spirit.[119] But it is clear that by *baptisma* Cyprian, like Tertullian, may be referring here to the whole baptismal complex including the laying on of hands, for elsewhere he says:

> They who are baptised in the Church are brought to the prelates of the Church, and by our prayers, and by the imposition of hands obtain the Holy Spirit ...[120]

[118] *initiorum Christi sermonem tenemus, tamquam parvuli...* ('we hold fast the discourse of the initial things of Christ, just like little children ...'). See *Homélies sur les Juges*, edited by Pierre Messié, Louis Neyrand & Marcel Borret, *Sources Chrétiennes* 389 (Paris, 1993). Origen speaks of the angels as guardians of the children of Christian parents in *Commentary on Matthew* 13.26-8, commenting on Matthew 18:10.

[119] Cyprian, *Epistles*. 63.8, 74.5 (62.8, 73.5 ANF); Lampe, *Seal of the Spirit*, p. 171.

[120] Cyprian, *Epistles* 73.9 (72.9 ANF quoted here). See 74.4 with its distinction between 'becoming God's temple' and 'the Holy Spirit being poured out upon the

He also speaks of the necessity of oil (chrism) for the baptised, saying that it confers the grace of Christ, though he does not elaborate further.[121]

Whilst emphatically asserting that baptism outside the Church is invalid, and that receiving schismatics and heretics into the Church merely by the laying on of hands (as Stephen, Bishop of Rome, required) is totally unsatisfactory because the baptismal complex cannot be divided, he can yet refer to baptism and the laying on of hands as two *sacramenta*.[122] The author of the near contemporary tract *On Rebaptism* goes further, making an explicit distinction between the 'baptism of water' and the 'baptism of the Spirit', stating that the bishop's laying on of hands may be separated from the water rite by an indefinite interval.[123]

Unlike Tertullian, Cyprian insists that baptism must not be withheld from even the youngest infant, for God's mercy and grace are for all. And he asserts that the Holy Spirit is given to them in no less measure than to adults.[124] He is also our first indubitable witness to infant communion.[125] But how is this to be reconciled with his statement elsewhere that it is *believers* who drink the cup, having received the Spirit in baptism?[126] Here we must concur with Lampe's verdict that Cyprian is guilty of 'rather muddled thought'.[127]

---

temple' which surely implies two steps in an initiation procedure; *pace* Lampe, *Seal of the Spirit*, p. 171.

[121] Cyprian, *Epistles* 70.2 (69.2 ANF).

[122] Cyprian, *Epistles* 71.1 (72.1 ANF).

[123] *On Rebaptism* 6, 10. See Lampe's discussion, *Seal of the Spirit*, p. 181.

[124] Cyprian, *Epistles* 64 (58 ANF).

[125] Cyprian, *On the Lapsed* 9, 25. For quotations and a brief discussion see Tommy Lee, 'The History of Paedocommunion from the Early Church until 1500' (c.1996), www.reformed.org/sacramentology (accessed December 2005), sections 5-6; Dalby, *Infant Communion*, pp. 10-11.

[126] Cyprian, *Epistles* 63.7-8 (62 ANF). No doubt this was overridden by his belief based on John 6:53 that reception of the eucharist was necessary to salvation (*On the Lord's Prayer* 18).

[127] Lampe, *Seal of the Spirit*, p. 170, though he is making a rather different point.

The Wider Patristic Scene

A glance at further developments within the Patristic Church reveals a bewildering diversity. Lampe tells us that it was their reverence for the Scriptures that led the Fathers of the Church from the third to the sixth centuries to ascribe the gift of the Spirit variously to the water rite, the anointing, or the laying on of hands, with little regard for consistency, just to suit the particular text they were dealing with at the time.[128] He can still find a considerable number of them who connect the Spirit primarily, it seems, with the water.

The importance of chrism in Christian initiation is nowhere more marked than in the Syrian churches. The earliest evidence comes from the third century when clearly the anointing preceded the water rite.[129] Jesus' baptism was taken as the prototype of every Christian initiation. As the Spirit came down on Jesus and empowered him to be the 'Anointed One' (Messiah) so from early times initiates were anointed with oil, perhaps at first symbolising, then regarded as conveying the gift of the Holy Spirit and entry to the messianic kingdom.[130] Fathers of the Eastern Church generally acknowledged the apostolic practice of laying on of hands, which persisted for a while, but 'sealing' the candidate with the sign of the cross by a presbyter using chrism blessed by a bishop was increasingly regarded as the particular moment when the Spirit was bestowed.[131]

In the Western Church this anointing (*consignatio*) along with the laying on of hands continued to be reserved for the bishop. As the number of parishes and converts grew so did the temporal separation of baptism, conducted by the presbyters, from the bishop's rites which, from the fifth century, began to be called *confirmatio*, referring to the

[128] Ibid., p.194.
[129] *Didascalia Apostolorum* 16, *Acts of Thomas* 121; but water baptism was not always considered necessary. See S.E. Myers 'Initiation by Anointing in Early Syriac-Speaking Christianity', *Studia Liturgica* 31 (2000), pp. 150-70.
[130] Bradshaw, *Christian Initiation*, ch. 7 is helpful here.
[131] Lampe, *Seal of the Spirit*, p. 265. The laying on of hands still has a significant place in initiation in the third-century Syrian church order *Didascalia Apostolorum* 9. Compare *Acts of Thomas* 49 (Greek).

'strengthening' of the candidate by the Holy Spirit.[132] With the growth of infant baptism this had one advantage – allowing the infants to approach an age of conscious faith and repentance, more ready for genuine commitment, more able to discern and reverently receive the body of Christ in communion.[133]

The catechumenate, involving an extended period of instruction before baptism, was particularly important in the fourth and fifth centuries, with the influx of large numbers of new converts into the Church after Christianity had been adopted as the religion of the Empire, but it subsequently declined with the growing prevalence of infant baptism.[134] That such instruction was important, however, was recognised by the sixteenth-century Reformers when they reintroduced a catechism before confirmation and subsequent admission to communion.

Conclusions

From the evidence we have considered we may draw three conclusions:

1. Whilst formally it may be true that, up to and including the time of Irenaeus, no contemporary initiation rite is mentioned apart from baptism in water, this cannot tell the whole story. That from a hitherto simple rite, suddenly, in the first years of the third century there sprang (through the reading of the Book of Acts) an initiation procedure of considerable complexity, is quite incredible. Irenaeus was himself quite familiar with Acts, and Tertullian and Hippolytus appear to be setting forth, in the main, already established baptismal procedures. It is then surely much more reasonable to conclude that, as Tertullian could use the term 'baptism' of a complex of rites, so could

---

[132] Lampe, *Seal of the Spirit*, p. 300. See J.D.C. Fisher, *Confirmation Then and Now*, Alcuin Club Collections 60 (London: SPCK, 1978), pp. 129ff.

[133] Dix, *Theology of Confirmation*, p. 31.

[134] A useful introduction to this subject is provided by Everett Ferguson in his article 'Catechesis, Catechumenate' in *Encyclopedia of Early Christianity* (2nd edition, New York: Garland, 1999), of which he is the editor.

earlier writers. For them, sometimes at least, 'baptism' or 'the water' was probably theological shorthand for a developing initiation rite, the elements of which varied somewhat in different parts of the Church. The laying on of hands, as a rite for the conferring of the Holy Spirit, could claim apostolic precedent. Even within the first century, in some of the Church at least, it had become a regular part of the initiation procedure, and so it continued and developed in the Western Church. Exactly when chrism became a regular element is unknown. Did it arise spontaneously somewhere to represent the baptismal candidate's counterpart of Christ being 'anointed by the Spirit' (Acts 10:38)? Was it adopted from Gnosticism? Did it stem ultimately from anointing for healing? We do not know. But in the Eastern Churches its association with the conferring of the Holy Spirit was strong enough for the laying on of hands to become quite early, it seems, redundant. With baptism in water the concepts of the washing away of sins and new birth remained inextricably bound.

2. That baptism is for those with faith (and repentance) is often indicated in the writings of the Fathers. The situation was, however, complicated by the practice of infant baptism. If, as our New Testament study in the previous chapter has shown, the gift of the Spirit was bestowed in response to faith-repentance, in what sense could baptised infants be said to receive the Spirit? Cyprian was surely wrong to maintain that they received no less of the Spirit than others. At their baptism, no doubt, through the prayers and faith of their sponsors, the Spirit began to work in their lives, setting their feet on the path of Christ. Even so, through life, they would need opportunities for conscious commitment to his cause, receiving then filling with his Spirit. Such an opportunity was offered later by the Reformers at confirmation at the 'years of discretion'.

3. St Paul had spoken of the need for discernment and reverence in those who participate in the Lord's Supper. That such participation was restricted to believers was

emphasised by the Fathers.[135] Again, it seems, infant baptism complicated the issue. Initially, as has been argued above, the Church may have been influenced by the Jewish practice for *bar mizwah* and delayed admission to communion until about the age of thirteen. What happened in the predominantly Gentile churches? It may be that practice varied considerably from place to place. The development of the catechumenate, however, shows how seriously the responsibility of instructing those *outside* the Church was taken before they were deemed ready to receive the privileges of membership. Is it not likely then that the children of those *within* also received instruction, at least in the earliest centuries, to avoid unworthy eucharistic participation? There are hints that this might have been so.[136] Whether or not it was the case, if in fact discernment and faith are important prerequisites for receiving communion, the Reformers' practice of delaying admission until after confirmation following catechetical instruction at the age of discretion was surely a step of great value.

---

135 Justin, 1 *Apology* 66, Cyprian, *Epistles* 70.2 (69.2 ANF).

136 Besides my comments above at the end of the section on Origen, consider *Didascalia Apostolorum* 9 where a considerable period of teaching would seem to intervene between baptism and partaking of the eucharist – only possible surely in the case of infant baptism. The passage runs as follows: 'But do you honour the bishops, who have loosed you from sins, who by the water regenerated you, who filled you with the Holy Spirit, who reared you with the word as with milk, who bred you up with doctrine, who confirmed you with admonition, and made you to partake of the holy Eucharist of God, and made you partakers and joint heirs of the promise of God'. Despite the assertions of Lee, 'History of Paedocommunion', section 12, and Dalby, *Infant Communion*, p. 10, that there is no straightforward chronological sequence in these statements since 'loosing from sins' precedes baptism etc, if one brackets certain clauses together: 2-4 (baptism), 5-7 (instruction), 8 (eucharist), 9 (the Christian hope), the passage still suggests a meaningful chronological progression.

CHAPTER FIVE
THE SIXTEENTH-CENTURY REFORM

To understand the changes in baptism, confirmation and admission to communion that were made in the sixteenth century (and completed in the seventeenth, when the 1662 revision of the Book of Common Prayer took place), one needs first to appreciate the situation in the late Middle Ages preceding the changes, as it had developed since the patristic period.

The practice of infant baptism was universal, and it was understood to impart to the infant spiritual regeneration and the forgiveness of sins *ex opere operato* ('as a result of the act performed'). Justification before God was likewise conferred in infant baptism, faith and repentance being supplied vicariously by the godparents. This teaching was confirmed by the Council of Trent in 1546 and 1547.[137]

Confirmation was administered by anointing, and because in the West it was administered by the bishop in person and not just with episcopally consecrated oil (as in the East), it had gradually become more and more customary for it to be delayed for a few years after baptism, except in the rare cases where the bishop himself was the baptiser. Originally it had been part of the baptismal rite, and in the East it still was. Since anointing symbolised the gift of the Spirit, theologians had been speculating about a second spiritual benefit, of strengthening, conferred in confirmation, and the rite had been reinterpreted as a separate sacrament (one of the mediaeval seven).[138]

Admission to communion sometimes took place at about the age of seven, followed by confirmation at about the age of eight, as is still the normal custom in the Church of

---

[137] In its decrees and canons on Original Sin and Justification.
[138] See J.D.C. Fisher, *Christian Initiation: Baptism in the Mediaeval West*, Alcuin Club Collections 47 (London: SPCK, 1965), ch. 8.

Rome. This curious inversion of order was due to the fact that, for many centuries from the mid-third century onwards, admission to communion had taken place in infancy, as it still does in the East; but in the thirteenth century the West had had second thoughts about this, being anxious for reverent treatment of the elements, and had deferred admission until an age of conscious awareness nearer the age of confirmation;[139] though only in England did it defer admission until *after* confirmation. The purpose of the English ruling was to prevent confirmation being neglected, though it had the additional effect of restoring the ancient order of events.[140]

The Reformation Changes

The changes to this pattern of theology and practice which were made by the sixteenth-century Reformers, and especially the English Reformers, are set out in a well-informed appendix to the 'Knaresborough' report *Communion before Confirmation?* written by the Rev. Martin Jackson. Unfortunately, his paper is not as well argued as it is well informed, and he charges the Reformers with fundamental inconsistency, a fault with which his own paper could much more truly be charged, as we shall see.

The Reformers took issue with several important points in this area of mediaeval teaching. As regards baptism, they were fully convinced, on the grounds of the analogy of circumcision and other arguments, of the right of infants to be baptised.[141] But, because of their recognition of the importance of personal faith as the means of appropriating

---

[139] Ibid., ch. 6; Dalby, *Infant Communion*, ch. 3. It is sometimes alleged that the advent of belief in transubstantiation was the only reason why infant communion was abandoned, but one did not need to believe in transubstantiation to see that it was undesirable for infants to cough up the wafer or splutter over the cup, not knowing what they were doing.

[140] This ruling was made at the 1281 Council of Lambeth, convened by Archbishop Peckham. His canon was incorporated into the Sarum Liturgy, and became the basis of the rubric concluding the Confirmation service in the Book of Common Prayer.

[141] For Cranmer's account of the grounds of infant baptism, see his treatise *A Confutation of Unwritten Verities*, ch. 10, in *Miscellaneous Writings and Letters of Thomas Cranmer* (Cambridge: Parker Society, 1846), p. 60.

justification before God, and of its strong link with baptism, they could not accept the proxy declaration of faith by the sponsors as more than a temporary substitute for it.[142] Luther, indeed, argued that faith was infused into the child at his baptism, but even Lutherans were not fully convinced by this, and there is no hint of it in the Augsburg Confession, where faith comes through the ministry of the word. The alternative was to make baptism efficacious to infants in so far as they are capable of it, but to delay its full efficacy until they are old enough to respond in faith to gospel teaching. This is the line taken by the English Reformers. Cranmer continued the proxy declarations of repentance and faith by the godparents, but understood them as a dramatic way of expressing the fact that the repentance and faith of the candidate are an essential part of baptism, even when the candidate is an infant.[143] This was underlined in the 1662 revision of Cranmer's service, immediately before the interrogation of the godparents, by stating that they were the candidate's sureties 'until he come of age to take it upon himself'. Similarly, in the Jacobean appendix to the Prayer Book Catechism, dealing with the sacraments, after stating that repentance and faith are required of candidates for baptism, and asking the pertinent question 'Why then are infants baptised, when by reason of their tender age they cannot perform it?' it answers 'Because they promise them both by their sureties: which promise, when they come to age, themselves are bound to perform'.

Because of this understanding of the role of personal faith in relation to baptism, Cranmer prefixed to the confirmation service provision for a personal ratification by the candidate of the undertakings made at his baptism by his godparents. He also deferred confirmation for some years, until such time as the candidate could say the Creed, the Lord's Prayer and the Ten Commandments, and could

---

142 For personal faith as the means of appropriating justification, see Romans 4; Galatians 3; Hebrews 10-11. For the link between faith and baptism, see Acts 19:4-5; Galatians 3:26-27; Colossians 2:12. See also the link between repentance and baptism in Acts 2:38.

143 *Writings and Disputations of Thomas Cranmer Relative to the Sacrament of the Lord's Supper* (Cambridge: Parker Society, 1844), p. 124f.

answer the questions about them in the newly drawn-up Catechism. He gave three reasons for making these changes, only one of which was retained by the cautious 1662 revisers of the service. It was the following:

> Because that when children come to the years of discretion, and have learned what their godfathers and godmothers promised for them in baptism, they may then themselves with their own mouth, and with their own consent, openly before the Church, ratify and confirm the same; and also promise that by the grace of God, they will evermore endeavour themselves faithfully to observe and keep such things, as they by their own mouth and confession have assented unto.[144]

Privately, of course, a Christian who has reached the age of discretion could exercise repentance and faith without publicly expressing it in this way. But since the New Testament calls on Christians to be willing to profess their faith openly (Matthew 10:32-33, Romans 10:9-10, 1 Timothy 6:12, 1 John 4:14-15) and since the profession of faith is in this case to lead to participation in the sacrament of holy communion, which is a corporate act of the church, the Prayer Book provision is right. At the baptism of an adult, the candidate would express his faith openly, as a visible sacrament, ministered by one Christian to another, necessarily requires; and in the case of one baptised as an infant, it is his delayed baptismal profession that he is now making at his confirmation.

Despite all this evidence to the contrary, Martin Jackson maintains that the Prayer Book adheres to the mediaeval notion of the adequacy of proxy professions, and therefore views infant baptism as complete in itself, without the candidate's subsequent profession of faith and repentance made in confirmation. If he had simply maintained that infant baptism was complete in *ceremonial* terms, without the anointing or imposition of hands which occurs in confirmation, this would be a much more defensible account of the Reformers' views. But to say that it is

[144] Book of Common Prayer 'The Order of Confirmation', introductory preface. The two other reasons alleged were the temptations of adolescence and the practice of the ancient church (see below).

complete as a *sacrament*, that is, complete in *spiritual* terms, without faith or repentance, is a travesty of the Reformers' teaching.

It is only because of his mistaken idea that in infant baptism the Reformers effectively dispensed with the need for personal faith that he can claim that, in consistency, they ought to have done the same in regard to the other sacrament, and recognised infant admission to holy communion. In making this claim, he involves himself in an inconsistency of his own, for the report to which he is contributing is not contending for the admission of infants but for the admission of young children – not for the Eastern Orthodox practice but for something much more like that of the Church of Rome.

To sum up, the teaching of the English Reformers is that baptism is not complete without personal faith and repentance, and that therefore infant baptism is not complete until the candidate has reached the age of discretion and has exercised faith and repentance in person, as at his confirmation. Until his baptism has been completed, it would be premature to admit him to the other sacrament. As Hooker says, baptism is for beginning the new life, and holy communion for continuing it, and they should not be confused.[145]

The Age of Confirmation

The 'years of discretion', to which the Prayer Book refers, are not an exact age, but were apparently understood at the time to mean between the ages of 12 and 15 – somewhat older than the phrase meant in mediaeval usage. In the 1603 Canons, young people are expected to become communicants by the age of sixteen.[146] In general, the age of

[145] Richard Hooker, *Laws of Ecclesiastical Polity* 5:67:1. It is with this distinction that Hooker opens his discussion of the eucharist.

[146] Canon 112. For the mediaeval usage of the phrase 'years/age of discretion', see Fisher, *Christian Initiation: the Reformation Period*, p. 238f. The phrase was first used of the age of admission to communion by the Fourth Lateran Council and later by the Council of Trent, but it was very variously interpreted. Sometimes it was taken to mean ages as late as 10 to 13, but nowadays it is understood to mean

confirmation in the Church of England has remained much the same as this, even though growing up is now perhaps a slower process.

The two other reasons which Cranmer gave in the first two Prayer Books for raising the age of confirmation to this level were the temptations of adolescence and the practice of the ancient church. The first of these reasons was derived from mediaeval sources and the second from Continental Protestantism. In so far as the first was valid, it suited the age of fifteen better than the age of eight. The validity of the second has been much disputed, and it would probably be more defensible in terms of the age of admission to communion (which seems to have been distinctly older in the period prior to the mid-third century) than in terms of the age of confirmation.[147] Both these reasons were dropped in the 1662 revision of the Prayer Book.

The Theology of Confirmation

The mediaeval conception of confirmation as a separate sacrament was firmly rejected by the Reformers. In the homily 'Of Common Prayer and Sacraments', included in the Second Book of Homilies, it is explained that only baptism and holy communion really fit the definition of a sacrament, as a visible sign, divinely commanded, with a promise of saving grace annexed to it. Though the other five of the mediaeval seven are retained in some form by the Church of England, and have certain characteristics in common with sacraments, they are in reality:

> for godly states of life, necessary in Christ's church, and therefore worthy to be set forth by public action and solemnity, by the ministry of the church; or else judged to be such ordinances as may make for the instruction, comfort, and edification of Christ's church.

Confirmation, which is separately described as

---

about 7; Heinrich Denzinger & Adolfus Schönmetzer (eds.), *Enchiridion Symbolorum* (36th edition, 1976), section 3530.

[147] For evidence of the beliefs of the Continental Reformers about ancient precedents for their confirmation practice, see Fisher, *Christian Initiation: the Reformation Period*, pp. 165-205.

> confirmation of children, by examining them of their knowledge in the articles of the faith, and joining thereto the prayers of the church for them

clearly belongs to the second of these two categories.

In the Elizabethan revision of the Thirty-nine Articles, confirmation is listed in Article 25 as one of the 'five commonly called sacraments', and a rather less positive, but basically similar, account of the five is given. They are said to be either 'states of life allowed in the Scriptures' (Orders and Matrimony) or 'such as have grown ... of the corrupt following of the Apostles' (Confirmation, Penance and Extreme Unction). The latter description is not *wholly* negative: the three practices have grown from a 'following of the Apostles', who laid hands on the baptised, remitted and retained sins, and anointed the sick, though the practices have become corrupt. In the case of confirmation, Cranmer's service also uses the significant words 'upon whom (after the example of thy holy Apostles) we have now laid our hands', thus emphasising its worthy origin. The corruptions, in the case of this service, would be the substitution of anointing for the laying-on of hands and, more importantly, the exaltation of a ceremony anciently appended to baptism, though without a divine command or promise, into a separate sacrament. The nature of the ceremony, as Cranmer interpreted it in the service, was an act of blessing: 'to certify them (by this sign) of thy favour and gracious goodness towards them'. So, although the service contains no *promise* of grace, it contains a *prayer* for grace; and the efficacy of the ceremony, as Cranmer states elsewhere, 'is of such value as is the prayer of the bishop in the name of the church'.[148] The Reformers judged it wisest, in the case of those baptised as infants, to delay this prayer until they had made the baptismal professions in their own name, and were ready to be admitted to holy communion.

Incidentally, Cranmer's Confirmation service retains the mediaeval language of 'strengthening', but probably uses it

[148] *Miscellaneous Writings and Letters,* p. 80. The similarity of Cranmer's account with the definition of confirmation in the homily will be noted.

in a different sense. His phrase 'Strengthen them, we beseech thee, O Lord, with the Holy Ghost the Comforter' would in the Middle Ages have meant 'Strengthen them by giving them the Holy Ghost', as Bernard Leeming shows, against Dix.[149] But since Cranmer deliberately substituted this phrase for the phrase 'Send upon them the sevenfold Holy Ghost' in the Sarum rite, it seems more likely that he simply means 'Strengthen them *through* the Holy Ghost'.

The Age of Admission to Communion

In the case of admission to holy communion, the Western reformers of the thirteenth century had delayed this until the age of conscious awareness, so the sixteenth-century Reformers completed the process. An age like seven was one at which only minimal instruction was possible, but at the 'years of discretion' (as the Reformers understood the phrase) they could learn the Creed, the Lord's Prayer and the Ten Commandments for themselves and be instructed in their meaning through an adequate Catechism, so as (hopefully) to be able to profess repentance and faith with sincerity and understanding when their confirmation and admission to communion came. The intellectual content of faith, as the Reformers looked for it on this occasion, was confined to basic truths. Far from being over-intellectual, as the advocates of child-communion usually allege, it was deliberately elementary.

In baptism, the requirement of faith and repentance could be deferred, because there was adequate evidence that the sacrament was intended for infants; the requirement could be deferred, but it could not be dispensed with, and at confirmation the age had arrived for the requirement to be fulfilled. In holy communion, on the other hand, there was no evidence that the sacrament was intended for infants: indeed, there was evidence that it was not, such as the use of wine. So the requirements made by our Lord at his

[149] Bernard Leeming, *Principles of Sacramental Theology* (new edition, London: Longmans, 1960), appendix 1.

institution of the sacrament, and by St Paul in his teaching about it, that it is to be celebrated in remembrance of the Lord's death, with a discerning of his body and with prior self-examination (Luke 22:19, 1 Corinthians 11:24-32), were intended to be fulfilled by all communicants on the occasion of the celebration and not at some future date. And it would be a suitable preparation for fulfilling these requirements, to make in one's own person the baptismal declarations of faith and repentance, by being confirmed.

The Reformers, therefore, guided as they were by Scripture, had a fully integrated and fully consistent theology and practice in regard to the sacraments, whatever their present-day critics may allege. It is the pattern which they established that we have inherited in the Church of England, and the sooner it is re-established in all dioceses and parishes, the better.

CHAPTER SIX
PASTORAL CONSIDERATIONS

The Reformation inherited a tradition of long services, which it did little at first to alter, as a glance at history will show.

The Historical Background to Present-Day Practice

After the Reformation, it became customary in the sixteenth and seventeenth centuries for Morning Prayer, with Litany, followed by Ante-Communion, to be read in parish churches every Sunday morning, with hardly a break between. Ante-Communion included provision for a sermon (usually of about an hour), and metrical psalms were added to the liturgical provision, in much the same way as hymns are added today. When the rest of the Communion service was included and the sacrament was administered, the service was, of course, longer still. Because of widespread illiteracy, the people's part of the service had, in many churches, to be said by rote after the parish clerk, which absorbed even more time. But on Sunday people were not busy.

Evening Prayer (often held in the afternoon, because of the inadequacy of artificial lighting) was a shorter service. The catechising of children took place on this occasion, and there might or might not be a sermon, as no rubric required it then. It was assumed that people would attend church both morning and evening.[150]

It was not until well into the Victorian period that desire for shorter services became widespread, and the Act of Uniformity Amendment Act, commonly known as the Shorter Services Act, was passed in 1872 to make lawful

[150] See, for example, George Herbert, *A Priest to the Temple, or the Country Parson* (written 1632), chs. 8, 21. All parishioners, and not just those being catechised, are expected to attend catechising, at Evening Prayer.

provision for this. But even up to the First World War, the long, composite Sunday morning service persisted in many places.[151]

The Reformers encouraged the administration of communion every Sunday, but they found that the laity, who had become accustomed in the Middle Ages to receiving it only once a year at Easter, were resistant to so great a change of practice. The Reformers were strongly opposed to the private mass, where the priest alone received, and to the notion that non-communicating attendance at the service by the laity offered them an alternative spiritual benefit, so they cancelled the Sunday celebration except when there were communicants ready to receive the sacrament with the priest. The result was that in many churches the sacrament was administered only once a month or even once a quarter,[152] but the Prayer Book ruled that the Ante-Communion was nevertheless to be read every Sunday, as a reminder of the desirability of more frequent reception. One of the exhortations provided in the service concentrates on precisely that issue. It was not until the Evangelical Revival of the eighteenth century that determined efforts were made to respond to this ideal: many of its leaders in that century and the early-nineteenth century emphasised that one of the principles of spiritual religion was a more frequent reception of communion.[153] Such numbers began to receive the sacrament that an early-morning celebration was added to make provision easier,[154] and though this was originally a supplementary celebration, it became in time the main one. Later in the nineteenth century, another supplementary celebration was added, after Evening Prayer, and though this began in High Church circles it became more popular in

[151] See S.C. Lowry, 'Our Sunday Services: are they too long?', *Churchman* 26 (May 1912).
[152] George Herbert (ch. 22) speaks of monthly celebrations, or at least five or six times a year, as appropriate.
[153] See Max Warren, *Strange Victory: A Study of the Holy Communion Service* (London: Canterbury Press, 1946), especially part 3, for an impressive collection of evidence.
[154] G.R. Balleine, *A History of the Evangelical Party in the Church of England* (London: Longmans, Green, 1911), p. 131.

Evangelical churches, where there was less concern for fasting reception of the sacrament.[155]

In the course of the nineteenth century, the Tractarian Movement added its own powerful voice in favour of frequent reception to the earlier Evangelical emphasis on it, and this extended the ideal to other circles of the Church of England. In reaction against Tractarianism, sadly, Evangelical enthusiasm for frequent reception somewhat waned.

The Parish Communion Movement

It was against this sort of background that the Parish Communion movement, prompted by the earlier Roman Catholic Liturgical Movement, became influential among Anglo-Catholics in the 1930s.[156] Their aim was to establish a celebration of the eucharist, with communicants, at about 9am on Sunday, in place of the earlier Anglo-Catholic pattern of an 8am celebration, with communicants, followed by a non-communicating high mass in the middle of the morning. It was thought that more would come at 9am than at 8am, especially if a parish breakfast followed the service, but that the hour was still early enough to make fasting reception practicable. (Since the relaxation of the Roman rules on fasting reception, which began in 1953, many Anglo-Catholics have felt less tied to 9am). Non-communicants also were encouraged to attend, so as to make the occasion, as far as possible, a meeting of the whole congregation; the furnishings were arranged in a more congregational manner; and the ceremonial was simplified for the benefit of newcomers and the young.

That the influence of the Parish Communion movement progressively extended outside Anglo-Catholic circles was

---

[155] Ibid., pp. 159-61.

[156] See especially Gabriel Hebert (ed.), *The Parish Communion* (London: SPCK, 1937). For the forerunner of the Parish Communion movement, the Liturgical Movement in the Church of Rome, see E.B. Koenker, *The Liturgical Renaissance in the Roman Catholic Church* (Chicago: University of Chicago Press, 1954). The *Constitution on the Sacred Liturgy* of the Second Vatican Council, approved in 1963, is of course an outcome of the Liturgical Movement.

due to a number of factors. One was that Anglo-Catholicism was then reaching its period of highest influence in the Church of England. A second factor was that the simplification of Anglo-Catholic worship and the movement away from the non-communicating mass made the new service-form more congenial to other schools of thought. A third factor was that the current enthusiasm for the Ecumenical Movement and Prayer Book revision made liturgical innovation more interesting and attractive. But perhaps the main factor was the uneasy conscience of Evangelicals about their latter-day lack of emphasis on the sacraments. An early-morning celebration of communion, or a shortened celebration as an optional extra after Morning or Evening Prayer, especially if not very well attended, appeared to have moved Holy Communion to the periphery of church life; and the fact that the celebration after Morning Prayer had for centuries been the main celebration was quite lost to sight. The Parish Communion movement certainly put Holy Communion back at the centre. Whether a better solution to the Evangelicals' problem might not have been to change their attitude to the sacraments, and to emphasise the importance of devoutly and frequently attending communion at the hours when it was available, as their forefathers had done, was a question which was not asked at the time but which needs to be asked now. Is it really desirable that everyone in the congregation, young and old, communicant and non-communicant, should be encouraged to come to one particular service on Sunday, a communion service, if there are other ways of emphasising the importance of the sacrament? For the consequences of emphasising it in this particular way have been serious.

1. It has given the impression that other services are unimportant, and so has increased the tendency of worshippers to attend church only once a Sunday, to the impoverishment of their spiritual lives.

2. It has created teaching difficulties, by bringing together adult Christians, children and fringe church-members, all to be taught together (unless separate

provision can be made for each group, which is not everywhere possible). To teach children at adult level, or adults at children's level, is bound to be unsatisfactory. The presence of children and a large number of communicants also restricts the time that can be given to teaching.

3. The Parish Communion has confronted fringe church-members with a dilemma: do they stay away, because they know that a communion service is for the committed, whereas they do not feel ready for more than simple instruction; or do they go and partake, although unprepared? To go, but not to partake, seems rather pointless, but to go and partake unworthily is spiritually dangerous, as they half-recognise.

4. Especially in country areas, where many churches can now have only one service a Sunday, that service always tends today to be Holy Communion, and thus is unsuitable for many parishioners.[157]

5. If it be asked, was it not the practice of the early church to invite everyone to the communion service? This is to forget that, in the discipline of the early church, non-communicants were required to leave before the administration of the sacrament.[158] That may not seem an appropriate requirement today, but without some suitable substitute confirmation–discipline tends to break down altogether.

6. In favour of the Parish Communion, it is sometimes argued that in New Testament times children must have attended the eucharist, since there is no evidence of separate provision for them. Actually, there is little evidence either way, but it must be remembered that the eucharist then took place in the context of the agape or love-feast, which was a provision of ordinary food, especially for Christians in need (children no doubt included). But that is not the context of

[157] Already by February 1988, this problem had become sufficiently serious for the House of Laity of the General Synod to pass, by a majority of 151 votes to 3, a motion calling for an adequate provision of non-eucharistic services in the parishes.
[158] See W.E. Scudamore, *The Communion of the Laity* (1855, reissued London: Skeffington, 1902).

the eucharist today. It is also argued that Jesus' welcoming attitude to children, and his setting of them as examples before his disciples, mean that their presence at the eucharist is even more appropriate than that of adults. But Jesus welcomed them to him in order to bless them (Mark 10:13-16), not to give them wine; and his choice of them for examples was probably intended to teach adults to trust their heavenly Father, as children trust their earthly parents and elders, rather than to say anything about the position of children in worship.

7. As the Parish Communion has caused many children to be brought to holy communion who would otherwise have attended Sunday School or Bible Class, this obliges one to ask, what is their part in the service? They can of course be blessed, as the children were by Jesus, but the fact that it is a communion service forces the question, can they not be given the sacrament? The existence of the Parish Communion thus turns a theoretical question into a practical one, which it otherwise would not be.

Of course, despite all these problems, the Parish Communion will not, after seventy years, be easily displaced. Among Anglo-Catholics, with whom it originated (and who, in fairness be it said, have tended to operate it in a much more disciplined way than other schools of thought), it may never be displaced. But there is no compelling reason why those who are not Anglo-Catholics should hesitate to return to the historic practice of the Church of England, with their eyes open to the danger of letting the sacrament be neglected. Simply to hold it at less frequented hours, such as after Morning Prayer or early in the day, is not in itself a token of neglect, since the sacrament is not intended for all churchgoers but is a privilege of the committed.[159]

[159] After Morning Prayer is a time when the Holy Communion has inevitably to be shortened, now that the stamina of worshippers is less than it was in the first few centuries after the Reformation. However, Morning Prayer can reasonably well do duty for the Ante-Communion, as it includes lessons, a creed, a sermon and intercessions.

There are, of course, other alternatives. The Parish Communion can be retained, but less exclusively: it can be held only on alternate Sunday mornings, or it can be alternated morning and evening. Teaching and evangelism can then be concentrated on the occasions when there is not a Parish Communion. The *Alternative Service Book 1980* and now *Common Worship* (2000) have provided a considerable measure of flexibility for such occasions. Baptisms, young people's parade services and Mothering Sunday all supply valuable opportunities for bringing the unchurched to worship. A non-eucharistic 'Service of the Word' can be tailor-made for parade services and Mothering Sunday, enabling all who attend to feel fully involved. The *Common Worship* Baptism service is substantial enough on its own to provide a main act of worship for the regular congregation and baptismal parties alike. To add a eucharist as part of these services would greatly lengthen them, and would also change their character: it is better omitted. For if the church is to address seriously the problem of declining numbers, it must not neglect its main times of Sunday worship as opportunities for evangelism.

The Question of Child-Communion

1. Against the background of the Parish Communion, the campaign for giving the sacrament to little children has been an almost inevitable development: the two can be separated, but both are really of Roman Catholic origin, and they belong naturally together. The Church of England's House of Bishops, to their credit, have not on the whole favoured the proposal of child-communion, and in the guidelines they have drawn up they treat it as exceptional, though they say that children who have once been admitted to communion should not be refused communion in any other parish.[160] Obviously, a move from a parish observing one discipline to a parish observing another is bound to involve a problem, but why the newcomer's past practice should automatically

[160] Guideline i or Revised Guideline j.

take precedence is difficult to see. The new incumbent would need to act with sensitivity, but a discussion with the child's family might lead to agreement on a different solution.

This is by no means the only pastoral problem which the admission of children to communion involves. It also involves the following.

2. As was said above, children attending communion are likely to be absent from Sunday School or Bible Class, and thus to cease getting instruction appropriate to their age. The obvious alternative is to address the instruction at the service to the children, but in that case the adults present cease to get instruction appropriate to their age.

3. If admission to communion is put years before confirmation, it becomes hard to persuade people of the necessity of being confirmed, as they found in the Middle Ages – hence Archbishop Peckham's canon. People naturally regard admission to communion as the chief benefit of confirmation: and are they wrong?[161] If the two were kept within a year of each other, and the first took place with the intention and expectation of going on to the second, as in the Church of Rome, the order would matter less. But to maintain such a link over six to eight years must be difficult almost to the point of being impossible.

4. If people stop getting confirmed, the bishop's only strong link with the laity of his diocese is destroyed. In an episcopal church, this is a very serious development.

5. Again, if people stop getting confirmed, confirmation preparation does not take place, which is one of the pastor's best opportunities of getting to know his people personally, instructing them appropriately and addressing their problems.

[161] The suggestion of the 'Knaresborough' report (p. 47) that admission to the electoral roll might become the new boon of confirmation, in place of admission to communion, ignores the fact that it is often hard enough to persuade people to join the electoral roll as things are, without putting the barrier of confirmation in their way.

6. A concern underlying the proposal of child-communion is the decline in the number of confirmation candidates, together with the large number of lapsed communicants.[162] But if the link between confirmation and admission to communion is broken, the decline in the number of confirmation candidates is bound to become still more serious. And if children cease to receive instruction appropriate to their age, or to experience confirmation preparation, the number of lapsed communicants is bound to become still greater.

So the problems involved in child-communion are not simply theological. It raises severe pastoral problems as well.

When all is said and done, the chief driving-force behind the attempted move from traditional Anglican practice to child-communion would seem to be a *sociological* one. In today's society, where the old authority-structures of the Victorian age have largely been discarded (not without some benefits, of course), parental discipline of children tends to be far less firm – indeed, many parents find it difficult to say "No!" to their children at all. This appears to be the case here too. One hears of children kneeling beside their parents and putting up their hands to receive, with the complaint "Why can't I have some?" And parents are slow to discourage them. Sometimes, conscious that their baptised children are within the New Covenant, parents actively want them to share in the sacred meal. We believe that children *can* be included, but in a different way, by receiving a blessing – in the same way as Jesus graciously blessed children brought to him. It should be explained to them, however, that receiving communion is a privilege worth waiting for until they are a little older, when the matter can be carefully explained and they can be confirmed. Such an approach surely makes them value the sacrament more. Of course, other church activities for children need to be provided, so as to maintain their interest until that time comes.

---

[162] *Communion before Confirmation?*, 'Knaresborough' report, p. 35.

CHAPTER SEVEN
CONCLUSION

1. The age of admission to communion is not a matter on which the Bible gives direct guidance. Three different ages have been customary in Christian history: infancy, known from the mid-third century in the West, and still observed in the East; childhood, observed from the thirteenth century in the West, and still observed in the Church of Rome; and adolescence, observed in the Churches of the Reformation.

2. The Jewish background to Christianity, and such evidence of Christian practice as exists from before the mid-third century, seems to indicate that adolescence was the original age of admission to communion, whereas infants probably began being admitted to baptism in apostolic times.

3. Confirmation originated as a ceremony closely linked to baptism, symbolising the baptismal gift of the Holy Spirit, and was only separated from it in the course of Western history. In the East, the close link remains, though the ceremony is one of anointing, not of the laying-on of hands. The laying-on of hands at confirmation appears to be a conscious imitation of an action of the apostles, though anointing was often added or substituted in patristic times.

4. The claim that baptism is 'complete Christian initiation' is therefore, in terms of New Testament and Early Church teaching, an overstatement. Baptism with water is the most important ceremony of initiation, but there are other related ceremonies, and though faith and the gift of the Spirit are closely connected to baptism, they do not invariably all occur together, as they are also closely connected to the ministry of the word.

5. The New Testament teaches that holy communion is to be celebrated in remembrance of Christ and his death, with a 'discerning of the body' and self-examination. There is no indication that these requirements can be waived or postponed.

6. The Reformers moved confirmation to the early teens, so that those baptised as infants could receive elementary Christian instruction and could then make the baptismal professions of faith and repentance in their own persons, immediately before being admitted to communion. Although the Reformers used confirmation for a new purpose, it was a purpose in general harmony with the New Testament and the primitive church, one which gave a renewed emphasis to repentance and faith, and completed what had been begun at baptism.

7. The Parish Communion movement, which owes its origin to the Roman Catholic Liturgical Movement and was pioneered in the Church of England by Anglo-Catholics, has brought renewal to Anglo-Catholic parishes but has been a mixed blessing in parishes of a more reformed tradition. Positively, it has reminded them of the importance of Holy Communion, but negatively, it has hindered teaching and evangelism, and has again forced upon the church the question of admitting children to communion at the mediaeval or Roman Catholic age.

8. Children are not adults but are at a stage of life that deserves recognition and respect for what it is. Having been baptised, their great need now is for elementary teaching. To hasten them to the other sacrament, and to defer confirmation until an age when they may never receive it, or even receive preparation for it, is to deprive them of what at their stage of life will most help them, and to hinder their prospects of reaching a mature faith, and of persevering as communicants.

9. By making confirmation more uncertain, child-communion also threatens the link between the bishop and the laity of his diocese.

We bring these points to the attention of the church today, with the earnest hope that they will be widely and seriously pondered. It would be a grave reversal if the church, without adequate consideration of the historical and theological issues involved, and guided mainly by the spirit of the age, returned to a pattern of pastoral practice which was for good reasons discarded no less than four and a half centuries ago.